Conformation

and Performance

CONFORMATION
AND PERFORMANCE

A GUIDE TO THE
PERFORMANCE CONSEQUENCES OF
COMMON CONFORMATION POINTS

BY NANCY S. LOVING, DVM
PHOTOGRAPHS BY BOB LANGRISH

02 01 00 99 98   9 8 7 6 5 4 3 2

For information address:
Breakthrough Publications
310 North Highland Ave.
Ossining, NY 10562
www.booksonhorses.com

Library of Congress Card Catalog Number: 97-076984

ISBN: 914327-75-5

Book cover and interior designed by
Greenboam & Company, Ossining, New York

Cover title type by Tricia Tanassy

Cover photograph by Bob Langrish

Diagrams of the Points, Bones, and Muscles of the Horse by Maria Belknap and Laurie Prindle.

Graphic annotations to photographs by Vernon Purdy

Impreso por:
Cargraphics S.A.-Imprelibros
Impreso en Colombia - Printed in Colombia

Contents

Introduction

The study of conformation typically evaluates the structure of a horse standing at rest, all four legs squared up on a level surface. This gives the examiner the opportunity to consider the various angles and proportions of an individual's body relative to itself and set against an ideal standard. However, the most important aspect of performance ability is how that horse moves and carries out the intended task. As riders, we seek a horse that moves with efficiency, agility, and a degree of elegance. In some cases, speed is the essential ingredient; in other instances, power is everything.

As you consider the photographs in this book and read the accompanying text, I would urge you to put each conformation characteristic into perspective. Rarely do we encounter a horse that matches an imaginary ideal. Yet, many a horse with imperfect structure is a tremendous athlete despite its structural shortcomings. A horse's standing conformation may have little bearing on its athletic prowess while in motion. Also, there is far more to performance success than being endowed with perfect conformation. A successful competition or pleasure horse must be fit and sound both in mind and body; a horse often excels because of "heart" or its determination to try.

A horse with a conformational flaw may not be affected in its work. One undesirable conformational characteristic may have limited impact if the rest of the horse is well put together or if the horse is used to its best advantage. As an example, a horse that travels light on its front end or participates in sports focusing more on effort from the hindquarters may never suffer ill effects from having a slightly crooked front leg. This book should help you decide what limitations your horse may have in certain athletics because of specific structural flaws, while allowing you to capitalize on the favorable attributes of your horse's structure.

In addition, I would caution anyone against breeding horses with lameness issues that have developed as a consequence of faulty conformation. Such a horse retired from performance may not be suitable as breeding stock if this perpetuates a conformational problem in the gene pool. The trick in achieving athletic longevity is to recognize a horse's lack of perfection at the onset, and to manage that horse within its genetic capacity to perform. Many problems can be headed off at the beginning before they develop to full blown lameness or behavioral issues.

Remember to watch each horse in motion to gain an understanding of its inherent athletic qualities. Only with this perspective will you be able to adequately evaluate a horse for ease of training and for excellence in your intended athletic pursuit.

Nancy S. Loving, DVM
April 1997

2

Points of the Horse

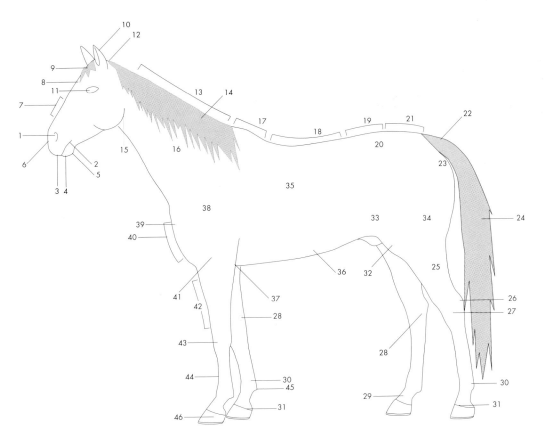

1 Nostril	19. Loin	37. Elbow
2. Mouth	20. Point of the Hip	38. Shoulder
3. Upper Lip	21. Croup	39. Point of the Shoulder
4. Lower Lip	22. Dock	40. Chest/Breast
5. Under Lip	23. Buttock	41. Arm
6. Muzzle	24. Tail	42. Forearm
7. Bridge of the Nose	25. Gaskin	43. Knee/Carpus
8. Forehead	26. Point of the Hock	44. Cannon
9. Forelock	27. Hock	45. Ergot
10. Ear	28. Chestnut	46. Hoof
11. Eye	29. Pastern	
12. Poll	30. Fetlock	
13. Crest	31. Coronet	
14. Mane	32. Stifle	
15. Throatlatch	33. Flank	
16. Neck	34. Thigh	
17. Withers	35. Barrel/Ribs	
18. Back (Upper)	36. Belly	

Points of the Horse—Front & Back

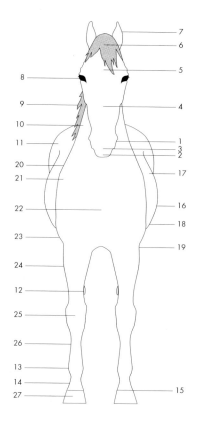

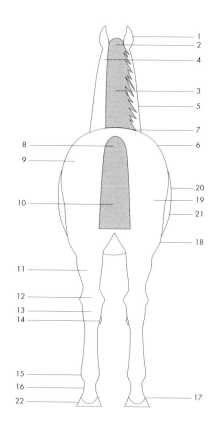

FRONT
1. Nostril
2. Upper Lip
3. Muzzle
4. Bridge of the Nose
5. Forehead
6. Forelock
7. Ear
8. Eye
9. Mane
10. Neck
11. Point of the Hip
12. Chestnut
13. Fetlock
14. Pastern
15. Coronet
16. Flank
17. Barrel/Ribs
18. Belly
19. Elbow
20. Shoulder
21. Point of the Shoulder
22. Chest/Breast
23. Arm
24. Forearm
25. Knee
26. Cannon
27. Hoof

BACK
1. Ear
2. Poll
3. Crest
4. Mane
5. Neck
6. Point of Hip
7. Croup
8. Dock
9. Buttock
10. Tail
11. Gaskin
12. Point of the Hock
13. Hock
14. Chestnut
15. Fetlock
16. Pastern
17. Coronet
18. Stifle
19. Thigh
20. Barrel/Ribs
21. Belly
22. Hoof

Bone Structure of the Horse

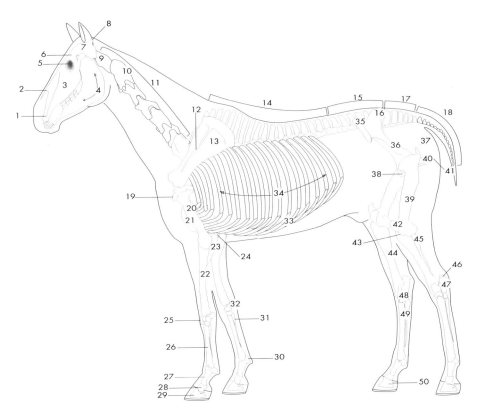

1. Premaxillary
2. Nasal
3. Maxillary
4. Mandible
5. Orbit
6. Frontal
7. Temporal Fossa
8. Occipitus
9. Atlas
10. Axis
11. Cervical Vertebra (7)
12. Scapular Spine
13. Scapula
14. Thoracic Vertebra (18)
15. Lumbar Vertebra (6)
16. Tuber Sacrale
17. Sacral Vertebrae (5)
18. Coccygeal Vertebrae (17-20)

19. Tuberosity of Humerus (Point of the Shoulder)
20. Humerus
21. Sternum
22. Radius
23. Ulna
24. Olecranon
25. Carpus
26. Large Metacarpus
27. 1st Phalanx (Long Pastern Bone)
28. 2nd Phalanx, Middle Phalanx (Short Pastern Bone)
29. 3rd Phalanx, Distal Phalanx (Pedal Bone)
30. Small Metacarpus
31. Proximal Sesamoid
32. Accessory Carpal
33. Costal Cartilages

34. Ribs (18)
35. Tuber Coxae
36. Ilium
37. Greater Trochanter of the Femur
38. Pubis
39. Femur
40. Ischium
41. Tuber Ischii
42. Patella
43. Femoral Trochlea
44. Tibia
45. Fibula
46. Tuber Calcanei (Point of the Hock)
47. Calcaneus
48. Talus (Tibial Tarsal)
49. Large Metatarsal
50. Distal Sesamoid Bone (Navicular Bone)

Muscles of the Horse

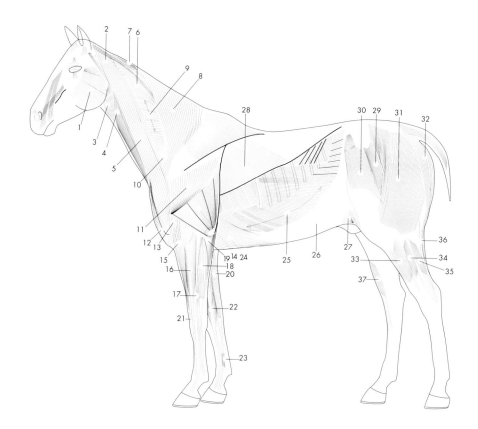

1. Masseter
2. Wing of the Atlas
3. Sternothyrohyoid/ Omohyoid
4. Sternocephalic
5. Brachiocephalic
6. Splenius
7. Rhomboid
8. Trapezius
9. Ventral Serate
10. Cranial Deep Pectoralis
11. Deltoid
12. Cranial Superficial Pectoral
13. Brachialis
14. Triceps
15. Radial Carpal Extensor

16. Common Digital Extensor
17. Lateral Digital Extensor
18. Lateral Carpal Flexor
19. Deep Digital Flexor
20. Middle Carpal Flexor
21. Oblique Carpal Extensor
22. Medial Carpal Flexor
23. Superficial Digital Flexor Tendon, Deep Digital Flexor Tendon, Suspensory Ligaments
24. Pectoral
25. External Abdominal Oblique
26. Aponeurosis of External Abdominal Oblique

27. Cutaneous
28. Latissimus Dorsi
29. Superficial Gluteal
30. M. Tensor Fascia Latae,
31. Biceps Femoris
32. Semitendinous
33. Long Digital Extensor
34. Lateral Digital Extensor
35. Deep Digital Flexor
36. Achilles Tendon
37. Anterior Tibial

Head and Neck

Dished Face

DESCRIPTION:
The face has a concave undulation or "dish" beneath the eyes that is often further exaggerated by a slightly bulging forehead (referred to as the jibbah).

HOW COMMON:
Common.

BREEDS/ACTIVITIES MOST AFFECTED:
Arabians and Arabian descent.

PERFORMANCE CONSEQUENCES:
• Any narrowing of the airway passages limits the airflow to the lungs and breathing capacity. Air and oxygen fuel muscle contraction and improve endurance and stamina. A dished face in the extreme has the potential to limit air flow with each inhalation, leading to exercise intolerance or poor staying power.
• A moderately bulging forehead (jibbah) presents a large diameter of the frontal bones beneath which lie the air-filled sinuses. A broad forehead provides proportionately more room for air exchange through the air passages. It provides a large surface area for attachment of facial muscles throughout the head that assist in opening the nostrils for air flow provided the dish below the eyes is not too pronounced.

MANAGEMENT/TRAINING STRATEGIES:
Conditioning and fitness improve overall cardiovascular, respiratory, and musculoskeletal efficiency so a horse is able to exercise for longer periods before feeling fatigued.

BEST JOB FOR THIS HORSE:
With proper conditioning, the horse should be able to participate in any sport, however slow, aerobic-type work that does not entail high speed galloping gives the horse the best opportunity to excel.

As seen in profile, this horse's face is slightly concave beneath the eyes. This is referred to as a dished face and is frequently found in the Arabian breed.

This horse appears to be in perfect health and in fact horses that are properly conditioned can take part in any discipline despite a dished face.

Small Nostrils

DESCRIPTION:
The opening of the nostrils, or nares, is narrow and somewhat restricted. This limits the horse's ability to expand the nostrils for inhaling and exhaling when exercising hard.

HOW COMMON:
Common.

BREEDS/ACTIVITIES MOST AFFECTED:
Any breed, any sport.

PERFORMANCE CONSEQUENCES:
• Any restriction of air and oxygen intake limits performance by insufficient supply of oxygen to fuel muscle contraction. This especially affects horses engaged in high-speed activities such as racing, eventing, steeplechase, or polo, or horses that need to sustain a work effort over a prolonged duration as seen with endurance riding, competitive trail, combined driving, or the roads and tracks phase of eventing.
• Small nostrils are often associated with a narrow muzzle and jaw that preclude ample room for chewing teeth and attachment of muscles of mastication that improve feed efficiency.

MANAGEMENT/TRAINING STRATEGIES:
Conditioning is exceptionally important in managing a horse with a small nostril as any strategy that minimizes muscular effort will improve endurance and stamina. Regular dental care promotes feed utilization to maintain body condition.

BEST JOB FOR THIS HORSE:
Pleasure riding, non-speed sports.

Left: Small nostrils mean smaller airways for breathing.

Below: This horse looks hale and hearty and proper care can keep him that way. Because small nostrils often go along with narrow jaws and muzzle, a horse's chewing teeth can be affected, so good dental care and overall conditioning are a must.

Photo by Nancy S. Loving, DVM

Steeplechasing, eventing, racing or polo are definitely not sports for horses with small nostrils. They are better suited to sports that involve limited galloping, such as pleasure riding.

Narrow Throatlatch/Narrow Jaw

DESCRIPTION:
To estimate the width of the jaw, touch the skin of the horse's neck with the back of your hand, then slide your flexed fingers forward between the wings of the jawbones, using the finger joint closest to the knuckles of your fist to measure. A jaw is considered narrow if this width measures less than four joints wide (average for Thoroughbreds), or less than 7.2 centimeters.

HOW COMMON: Common.

BREEDS/ACTIVITIES MOST AFFECTED:
Thoroughbreds and standardbreds; racing and speed horses such as flat track racing, steeplechase, timber, eventing, and polo.

PERFORMANCE CONSEQUENCES:
• To fuel muscle contraction, a horse must take in adequate air and oxygen. A horse with a narrow throatlatch may suffer from a restricted upper airway or air turbulence due to paralysis of the recurrent laryngeal nerve (RLN) ,which governs opening of the laryngeal cartilage. Horses affected by paralysis of one or both branches of the RLN make a roaring noise on inhalation at fast speeds because the laryngeal cartilage collapses into the airway space. Difficulty in obtaining sufficient air makes these horses exercise-intolerant particularly in speed work and may induce a horse to run-out or stop at fences due to hastened muscular fatigue. Airway turbulence is also thought to be associated with EIPH (exercise induced pulmonary hemorrhage); a horse with this problem is known as a "bleeder."
• A dressage horse or horse that is asked to go on the bit in a collected frame may be resistant to flexing at the poll as this further narrows the throatlatch and airway, further restricting sufficient airflow to support the work effort. The horse does not need to exhibit a roaring noise to still be affected by partial suffocation. These horses are known to be resistant in the bridle, tend to brace through the poll, neck, and back, and are difficult to train to upper levels of performance.

MANAGEMENT/TRAINING STRATEGIES:
Conditioning and fitness can only do so much to improve muscular efficiency. An endoscopic exam of a horse exercising on a high-speed treadmill may reveal mild paralysis of the laryngeal cartilages that could affect performance. Surgery should be performed to correct paralysis of the RLN and other associated syndromes such as dorsal displacement of the soft palate or epiglottal entrapment before one can expect a horse to perform to potential. If surgery is not an option, the horse should not be asked to perform in high-speed efforts like racing, eventing, or polo.

BEST JOB FOR THIS HORSE:
All sports that do not require gallop speeds are acceptable.

A narrow throat latch and jaw restrict a horse's ability to take in proper amounts of oxygen for strenuous workouts.

Photo by Nancy S. Loving, DVM

RLN can be corrected by surgery, but conditioning alone will do little to help. If surgery isn't an option a horse with a narrow throat latch or jaw is better sticking with sports that don't involve routine galloping.

If your horse makes a roaring noise when he works at the gallop he may suffer from paralysis of the recurrent laryngeal nerve·(RLN). This condition is often found in Thoroughbreds.

Wide Throatlatch/Wide Jaw

DESCRIPTION:
The throatlatch has sufficient space between the jaw bones allowing more than 4 finger joints to comfortably fit, and measuring greater than 7.2 centimeters.

HOW COMMON:
Common.

BREEDS/ACTIVITIES MOST AFFECTED:
Quarter Horses often have wide jowls, as do many Arabians.

PERFORMANCE CONSEQUENCES:
• Historically, a wide or thick throatlatch or jaw was thought to make a horse's head and neck less flexible, making flexion at the poll more difficult. In fact, a wide jaw or thick throatlatch poses no limitation on a horse's ability to accept the bit, flex the poll, and flex through the withers and back to engage the hindquarters. The broad area of the jaw also provides a large surface area for insertion of neck muscles that control equilibrium and rapid movement changes of the body.
• The large cross-sectional area in the region of the larynx, or voice box, should offer no limitation on air flow through the upper airways no matter what position the horse holds its head. Optimum air flow encourages optimum performance.
• Broad jaws provide a large surface area for attachment of the muscles of mastication and ample space for cheek teeth so important to obtaining adequate nutrition. These features are important in maintaining the body condition and health of a performance horse.

MANAGEMENT/TRAINING STRATEGIES:
Nothing special is required except to take advantage of the horse's inherent ability to inhale air and oxygen. Suppling exercises (lateral flexion) are always beneficial to increase bending flexibility side-to-side, while stretches encouraged under saddle increase flexibility of the head, neck, and spine.

BEST JOB FOR THIS HORSE:
Anything.

Quarter horses are often born with wide jaws. The benefits of such a build are many and a horse like this one should be able to compete in any discipline in terms of his ability to take in air, as long as he is properly conditioned.

Historically, a wide jaw was associated with a limited ability to flex and accept the bit. In fact flexion is not at all affected by this trait as is clearly demonstrated by this horse performing at top level dressage.

We see here a beautiful demonstration of the piaffe, a collected trot done in place, that requires extreme flexion and is performed by horses talented enough to compete at Grand Prix level dressage.

Short Neck

DESCRIPTION:
The ideal neck is proportional to the body, generally making up about one-third the horse's overall length. Neck length is measured from the poll to the withers and its length is often comparable to the length of the legs. A short neck is a relatively subjective determination as current breeding for show horses has increased the emphasis on length relative to what was popular by standards of past decades.

HOW COMMON: Common.

BREEDS/ACTIVITIES MOST AFFECTED: Any breed.

PERFORMANCE CONSEQUENCES:
• Contrary to popular opinion, a short neck is quite flexible despite appearing thick and muscular. Length and distance between cervical vertebrae may be somewhat reduced, yet function and range of motion are rarely altered. A horse may be slightly less flexible through the poll than a longer necked horse, but maneuverability and agility are not affected. Muscles of the neck extend into the shoulders and breast to draw the shoulder and forelimbs forward no matter the length of the neck.
• Length of stride has often been associated with the reach of the forelimbs to the tip of the nose, and this length depends on length of the neck. Neck muscles are able to contract two-thirds of their length; with that in mind, it would seem that a short neck and therefore a shorter reach would reduce a horse's stride. However, consider the extended trot of a dressage horse in collection where the front hooves reach way past the horse's nose despite the neck and head being held in a collected frame. This concept of restricted stride length may have some limited application for a race horse at full gallop plummeting toward the finish line. Actually, stride length has more to do with shoulder length and the angle created by the scapula and arm bone. The maximum distance the foot is able to reach is the point on the ground that arises from an imaginary line drawn through the slope of the shoulder to the ground. (Refer to Sloping Shoulder for detail.)

MANAGEMENT/TRAINING STRATEGIES:
Stretching exercises of the neck and back maintain flexibility through the spine from head to haunches, enabling any horse to use its head and neck to balance well. The rider should be skilled at a balanced seat so as not to throw unnecessary weight onto the horse's forehand.

BEST JOB FOR THIS HORSE:
A short-necked horse is capable of performing just about any sport, but may not excel as well in jumping high obstacles or galloping at top speeds.

A horse's neck size is measured in comparison to his overall body size. A properly proportioned neck should be approximately 1/3 of the horse's overall length. This horse's neck is a little on the short side which may cause him to be heavy on the front end. A rider with a balanced seat can help a horse that is short necked.

While a horse's stride length isn't affected by neck length, a short-necked horse may not be as handy at performing quick changes of direction, such as are required in barrel racing.

This horse is performing an extended trot out of collection and yet is able to get a long stride. Stride length is thought to be more affected by shoulder length than neck length.

Long Neck

DESCRIPTION:
A neck is considered long when its length exceeds the length of the horse's body, and is too long when its length approximates one and one-half times or more of the body length.

HOW COMMON:
Common.

BREEDS/ACTIVITIES MOST AFFECTED:
Thoroughbreds, Saddlebreds, Gaited horses.

PERFORMANCE CONSEQUENCES:
• The head and neck serve as a counterbalance to the body to control rapid changes in direction. A long neck adds nothing to improve a horse's balance but instead creates a liability because lengthy neck muscles are more difficult to develop in size and in strength. A horse with a long neck may fatigue more quickly with strenuous exercise, resulting in more weight falling onto the forehand. (Refer to Downhill Balance for more detail.) A long-necked horse needs broad withers to support the weight of the head and neck.
• The under-developed musculature common to a long neck often tends to become stiff and rigid, with the horse resistant and unyielding to the rider's aids. In horses with overly long necks, it is easier for the horse to bend its neck into an S-curve than to come through the bridle; this causes a horse to "fall" onto the inside shoulder and makes it difficult for the rider to straighten the horse. Such crookedness hinders excellence in dressage, equitation, and show performance and renders a horse less enjoyable to ride.
• A long, slender neck has been known to be associated with Wobbler syndrome (cervical vertebral malformation). Narrowing of the vertebral canal compresses the spinal cord which results in incoordination and serious neurological instability, rendering the horse unfit for riding.
• A long, slender neck is also associated with a narrow throatlatch with its accompanying problems of laryngeal paralysis. (See Narrow Throatlatch for more detail.)

MANAGEMENT/TRAINING STRATEGIES:
Straightening exercises promote flexibility and suppleness with the slightest hand and leg aids. This strategy prevents a horse from overusing one side of its body and creating lameness problems.

BEST JOB FOR THIS HORSE:
Jumping or speed sports, straight line riding such as trail riding.

A horse is considered long-necked if the length of his neck exceeds the length of his body, measured from withers to croup. If the neck is too long meaning that it is more than 1 1/2 times the length of his body, he may have trouble balancing and carry too much weight on his front end.

This horse may have difficulty performing in the dressage ring where collection is key because of his long neck. He may tend to carry his head and neck in an S-curve rather than work on the bit. When this happens he falls onto the inside shoulder instead of going straight.

The long-necked horse is best suited to disciplines like jumping or racing where there are no quick changes of direction.

Excessively Large Crest/Fallen Crest

DESCRIPTION:
An overly large crest gives a Trojan horse appearance to the top line of the neck. In extreme cases, the crest may "fall" to one side.

HOW COMMON:
Uncommon.

BREEDS/ACTIVITIES MOST AFFECTED:
Any horse can develop this, but it is more commonly seen in stallions, ponies, draft breeds, and Morgans.

PERFORMANCE CONSEQUENCES:
• A high, thick crest is often a result of excess deposits of fat above the nuchal ligament of the neck of an obese horse. Not only is this aesthetically displeasing, but the added weight of the neck places more weight on the forehand of the horse.
• The fat deposits in the neck represent an obese body condition that is not compatible with any state of fitness. Additionally, the state of a fat body condition poses multiple health risks to the horse:

  1. An overweight horse places undue stress on its own musculoskeletal structures. 2. A fat horse is at risk of developing laminitis. 3. A fat horse has trouble dissipating body heat upon exertion, therefore fatigues more rapidly and is prone to tying-up. 4. A fat horse is at risk of developing strangulating lipomas associated with fatal colic.

MANAGEMENT/TRAINING STRATEGIES:
A balanced diet and routine exercise are essential to bringing the horse's body condition back to normal. Consult your veterinarian for a safe strategy. A stallion or very old horse may still retain a large crest despite good conditioning, but fat deposits around the shoulders, withers, ribs, and rump should turn to sleek muscle with exercise.

BEST JOB FOR THIS HORSE:
An obese horse should only be ridden at slow paces (pleasure riding) to start so as not to overtax the musculoskeletal system or the horse's ability to dissipate body heat from muscle exertion. Once the horse reaches a moderate level of fitness, any sport can be undertaken.

A horse with a crest this large is probably overweight. In extreme cases the crest or top line of the neck may actually fall to one side because of the excess weight. Morgans, ponies, draft horses and stallions are most prone to this condition.

Bull Neck

DESCRIPTION:
A bull neck is so named because it is short and thick with a short upper curve. Its attachment to the body arises beneath a point half-way down the length of the shoulder.

HOW COMMON:
Fairly common.

BREEDS/ACTIVITIES MOST AFFECTED:
Draft breeds, Quarter Horses, and Morgans.

PERFORMANCE CONSEQUENCES:
• Such a thick, beefy neck makes it more difficult for the horse to maintain its balance if a rider is large or heavy, or if the rider is off balance. The rider may interfere with the horse's movement, causing a saddle horse to "fall" on the forehand, interfering with speed and agility. Without a rider mounted, a bull-necked horse would do fine if left to its own devices.
• For draft horses or carriage horses, a thick neck is desirable to provide comfortable placement of the collar. And, heavy muscles of the neck draw the forelimbs forward to generate pulling power.

MANAGEMENT/TRAINING STRATEGIES:
Stretching exercises under saddle, such as riding the horse in a long and low frame, improve suppleness of the neck and back. Bending exercises side-to-side also improve suppleness in the neck and shoulders.

BEST JOB FOR THIS HORSE:
Non-speed sports.

A bull neck is so named because of its strong, upper curve and short, thick appearance. Left on his own such a horse has no problems in range of motion, but with an inexperienced rider mounted he may tend to fall on his forehand.

The best way to condition a thick-necked horse is to work him in a low, long frame. Bending and flexing side-to-side will also help to make him more supple.

Draft horses commonly have short, thick necks and in fact such conformation is desirable for a horse that works in a head collar.

Ewe or Upside-Down Neck

DESCRIPTION:
Reminiscent of the shape of a sheep's neck, a ewe neck on a horse is poorly muscled across the topline with a noticeable dip in the neck just in front of the withers while the muscles on the bottom aspect of the neck are bulging and overdeveloped.

HOW COMMON: Common.

BREEDS/ACTIVITIES MOST AFFECTED: Any breed, but often associated with a long-necked horse. Affects performance in all sports, particularly dressage and jumping.

PERFORMANCE CONSEQUENCES:
• The bulging muscles on the bottom of the neck represent hypertrophy from overuse in a horse that holds its head high (stargazing) with neck in an "upside down" and extended position. The ewe neck has several negative effects on performance:
   1. It is difficult for the rider to control the horse as it braces against the bit with head and neck held high. This causes the bit to miss contacting the bars of the mouth so the rider can exert only minimal control and brakes. Such a horse becomes quite hard-mouthed. 2. The high head and neck carriage are counterproductive to movements of collection and to proper gait transitions. The horse not only elevates and extends the head, but there is no connection between the front end, the back, and the hindquarters. The horse then moves in a disjointed rhythm unable to elevate its back. Loins and lower back muscles may become sore. 3. The horse's vision is restricted when its head is held high (as compared to the ideal position when the head is held at a 45-degree angle to ground), so it is likely to trip and stumble and perhaps fall.
• The dip evident in front of the withers ("sunken crest") may indicate a lack of conditioning and muscle development in a young horse, an undernourished horse, or a horse left idle for too many years. This dip often fills in as the horse is ridden correctly into the bridle while using its back and abdominal muscles to advance the limbs. However, any bulging on the under-side of the neck should alert you to a tendency of the horse to "stargaze," making for an unpleasant ride and a horse that is difficult to train as described above.

MANAGEMENT/TRAINING STRATEGIES:
Suppling and flexing exercises, stretching exercises through the topline, and lateral exercises to improve use of shoulders and spine all aid the horse in finding a more correct way to balance its body and to accept bit contact by activating its neck and back. The horse should be ridden "long and low" to encourage proper muscle development and stretching of the top muscles of the neck.

BEST JOB FOR THIS HORSE:
Performance in any sport will be limited until carriage is corrected.

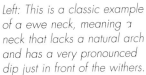

Left: This is a classic example of a ewe neck, meaning a neck that lacks a natural arch and has a very pronounced dip just in front of the withers.

Center: A dip in front of the withers may signal a horse that is underworked or underfed. A ewe neck may be improved through proper diet and flexing and suppling exercises.

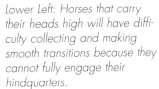

Lower Left: Horses that carry their heads high will have difficulty collecting and making smooth transitions because they cannot fully engage their hindquarters.

Lower Right: This horse's neck appears almost upside-down because the arch usually found along the topline is missing and instead the horse has developed a bulge on the underside. A strongly developed bulge is characteristic of a horse that is a "stargazer" and may be difficult to train to work in a frame.

Swan Neck

DESCRIPTION:
While being slender and relatively long, the upper curve of the neck is arched, yet a dip remains in front of the withers and the muscles bulge on the underside of the neck.

HOW COMMON:
Common.

BREEDS/ACTIVITIES MOST AFFECTED:
Saddlebreds, Gaited horses, Thoroughbreds.

PERFORMANCE CONSEQUENCES:
• The arch of the neck and the set of the neck coming out higher than halfway up the shoulder make it easier for this kind of horse to elevate its trunk and shoulders, giving a more floating stride especially at canter. This makes for a comfortable ride, but is not necessarily advantageous for speed.
• The length and arch of the swan neck makes it easy for a horse to lean on the bit and curl its nose to its chest without activating the back muscles. This affects dressage and show pursuits.

MANAGEMENT/TRAINING STRATEGIES:
Lengthening exercises through the neck and back while under saddle (ride the horse "long and low") prevent bracing against the rider's hands and the associated curling of the nose to the chest. Lateral work and lateral neck flexion exercises soften the horse at the poll and increase sensitivity to hand aids. Development of back and abdominal muscles "lifts" the horse off its forehand so it is less likely to curl its neck.

BEST JOB FOR THIS HORSE:
Showing, jumping, driving in harness, dressage.

Left: A swan neck is long and slender, but like the ewe neck dips in front of the withers. A horse built like this may give you a comfortable ride, but is not necessarily built for speed.

Center: A horse with a swan neck often leans on the bit and tucks his head into his chest without ever really collecting and working on the bit.

Lower Left: This horse appears to be very stiff through the neck. Lateral exercises and exercises that help him to flex and soften at the poll will better enable him to work on the bit and in collection.

Lower Right: The underside of this horse's neck is clearly overdeveloped and he appears to be bracing against the rider's hands and falling on his front end. Exercises that develop his back and abdominal muscles will help lift a horse off his forehand.

Photo by Nancy S. Loving, DVM

Photos by Nancy S. Loving, DVM

27

Arched or Turned-Over Neck

DESCRIPTION:
The crest of the neck is convex or arched with proportional development of all muscles of the neck so that none are excessive or lacking in substance.

HOW COMMON:
Common.

BREEDS/ACTIVITIES MOST AFFECTED:
Affects all breeds and all sports.

PERFORMANCE CONSEQUENCES:
• An arched neck has a crest that carries well back over the withers that appears as if the neck flows through to the center of the horse's back. This is not only aesthetically pleasing, but creates an efficient lever and balance arm for maneuvering, making this horse suitable for jumping activities, stock horse events that require sudden changes in direction, speed events, and polo.
• The strength of an arched neck with proportionate muscle development of top, middle, and bottom muscles improves the swing of the shoulder, elevates the shoulder and body, and aids the horse in engaging its hindquarters through elevation and activation of the back muscles. Dressage, driving, and long-distance trail riding are all sports well suited to a horse with an arched neck.

MANAGEMENT/TRAINING STRATEGIES:
Develop the inherent athletic capabilities of the horse through conditioning and training strategies for the work intended.

BEST JOB FOR THIS HORSE:
Anything.

Ideally you want a horse with a neck like this one that is nicely arched and proportionately developed through the top, middle and bottom. His neck gives the impression that it reaches back all the way through his withers and into his back.

This horse is beautifully executing a collected canter. His well-proportioned neck helps to balance him so he can properly engage his hind end and collect.

This equitation rider is working her horse on the bit. Notice how his arched neck helps balance him while the rider's contact at the bit encourages him to work from behind rather than brace against the bit.

Knife-Necked

DESCRIPTION:
Long, skinny neck with poor muscular development on both top and bottom aspects, giving the appearance of a straight crest with not much substance below.

HOW COMMON:
Uncommon.

BREEDS/ACTIVITIES MOST AFFECTED:
Any breed can be affected.

PERFORMANCE CONSEQUENCES:
• This neck is often associated with poor development of neck, back, abdominal, and haunch muscles, with the horse allowed to move in a strung-out frame, with no collection, often heavily weighting the forehand. This neck configuration is often rider-induced and not directly a product of underlying bone and muscle structure. A horse ridden with no collection work will be weak and will fatigue easily with the weight of the rider on its back.
• A horse with poor body development indicates a lack of inherent athletic ability. Such a mount requires more time and financial investment to "train" it to be athletic since that quality does not come naturally.

MANAGEMENT/TRAINING STRATEGIES:
Improvement of rider's riding skills and professional training to assist the horse in better using its body and finding its balance.

BEST JOB FOR THIS HORSE:
Light pleasure or trail riding until better skills and strength are developed.

A long, skinny neck is usually the sign of a horse that has not been properly conditioned. A rider with poor skills who allows a horse to only work strung out with no collection won't help him improve his musculature.

A horse born with a knife neck probably is not inherently athletic but with expert training can learn how to better use his body and balance.

Horizontal Neck

DESCRIPTION:
A horizontal neck is set on the chest neither too high nor too low with its weight and balance aligned with forward movement of the body.

HOW COMMON:
Uncommon.

BREEDS/ACTIVITIES MOST AFFECTED:
Thoroughbreds, Quarter Horses, some Warmbloods. Advantageous to every imaginable equestrian sport.

PERFORMANCE CONSEQUENCES:
• A horizontal neck is flexible and works well as a balancing arm to accommodate quick changes in direction common to polo or stock horse work like reining, cutting, roping, and gymkhana.
• A horizontal neck is neither too bulky or too thin, nor too long or too short. By virtue of its correct proportions such a neck is easy to supple, easy to develop strength and muscling, and easy for the rider to control through hand and leg aids in dressage. A horizontal neck confers speed for racing, polo, steeplechase, hunting, and eventing.

MANAGEMENT/TRAINING STRATEGIES:
Develop the inherent athletic talent of the individual.

BEST JOB FOR THIS HORSE:
Any equestrian sport, including speed events, stock horse work, and jumping.

Right: A horizontal neck is neither too bulky nor too thin, too high, or too low. It is ideal for almost any discipline, working as a balancing arm and allowing a horse to shift its weight forward and backward as needed. The feature is an advantage for travel at high speeds.

Above: Sports like polo or reining are no problem for the horse with a horizontal neck. He is well-balanced and thus able to make quick changes of direction.

Above: In a sport such as eventing you want a horse that is able to work powerfully from his hind end. This horse, with his well-proportioned neck will find balance and strength come naturally.

Conformation in Motion

Section 2
Body:
Withers, Back, Loins, and Croup

Mutton Withers

DESCRIPTION:
Mutton withers are flat and wide withers, created by relatively short spines projecting off the eighth through twelfth thoracic vertebrae.

HOW COMMON: Fairly common.

BREEDS/ACTIVITIES MOST AFFECTED:
Any breed may be affected, but often seen in Arabians and Quarter Horses. Affects all performance activities.

PERFORMANCE CONSEQUENCES:
• The withers form an important attachment point for muscles and ligaments that are responsible for extending the head and neck, extending the shoulder forward, and extending the vertebrae along the back, as well as providing an insertion point for muscles that open the ribs for breathing. A horse with short, mutton-shaped withers has less range of motion when extending its head and back muscles, causing the horse to be less able to elevate its back when the head and neck are lowered or extended. This limits the ability to engage the haunches so important to collection (dressage), jumping, and stock work.
• Thick, flat withers make it difficult to hold a saddle in place on a horse's back as it tends to slide forward moving the rider's weight more onto a horse's forehand. This interferes with a horse's balance while increasing concussion on the front end, affecting trail riding, stock work, jumping, eventing, or any sports in which a horse works over uneven terrain. Shoulder excursion is restricted by saddle/rider movement causing a horse to shorten its stride with the potential to interfere or forge. A horse with restricted movement may develop back pain.
• Because of limited definition between the neck and withers, a horse with this conformation would be difficult to fit well in driving harness using a collar as the collar would not "seat" as well into the groove of the neck without a defined withers as a backstop.

MANAGEMENT/TRAINING STRATEGIES:
The withers fully develop by age 5–6 so in some cases a very young horse with low withers may need more time to mature before being put into heavy saddle work. More efforts will be needed at developing haunch and abdominal muscles to assist the back in elevating for collected work. Hill climbs, trotting cavallettis, and jumping gymnastic grid exercises are exercises to use for muscle strengthening these body areas. To prevent forward motion of the saddle, use a crupper. Correct saddle fit is critical to the horse's comfort; one designed with wide, squared cutout at the pommel is best.

BEST JOB FOR THIS HORSE:
Pleasure riding, sports with minimal terrain changes, non-jumping activities.

Left: As you can see in this profile, this horse's withers are flat and wide, or mutton-shaped. There is almost no definition between his neck and his withers.

Above: In a sport such as barrel racing where good balance is critical, a horse with flat withers may have difficulty because of the saddle slipping, throwing the rider's weight onto the horse's forehand.

Above: Flat withers make it hard to hold a saddle in place. Without a crupper to secure it, the saddle will tend to slip forward moving the rider's weight to the horse's front end and impairing his balance.

Hollow Behind Withers

DESCRIPTION:
A "shelf" behind the withers gives a hollow appearance in that area, and is often created by a lack of muscular development.

HOW COMMON:
Common.

BREEDS/ACTIVITIES MOST AFFECTED:
High-withered horses of any breed. Affects all performance activities, especially dressage, jumping, speed events.

PERFORMANCE CONSEQUENCES:
• A hollow shelf behind the withers implies a less-developed muscular bed for the saddle to rest upon. Often a saddle will "bridge" in this area to pinch the withers and create soreness of the withers and surrounding muscles. Because of the pain and discomfort, the horse is less willing to move out or to extend its shoulders or use its back, especially for speed or jumping activities. Pain from the saddle will also prevent a horse from elevating its back and achieving true collection.
• Horses that tend to trot fast with the neck and head held in an erect position do not develop strong, active back muscles. Often a hollow is noted behind and just below the withers due to lack of collection. This is commonly rider-induced because the horse is allowed to move stiffly and strung out behind. This tendency particularly applies to distance trail horses and gaited horses. It is a tip off of incorrect body carriage that may require greater effort in training the horse.
• Protective movement by a horse to minimize saddle pinching may contribute to back pain. Persistent body carriage with lack of collection can overuse some musculoskeletal structures and lead to arthritis.

MANAGEMENT/TRAINING STRATEGIES:
It is critical to find a proper fitting saddle for this horse even if it needs to be custom made. Sometimes the musculature behind the withers can be developed through correct riding techniques that activate the back and abdominal muscles, but in some cases the bony protrusions off the spine dictate the shape of muscular attachments with limited ability to reconfigure them despite proper exercise. Maintaining a good body weight (fat) on the horse will help. Use a pad under the saddle to relieve pinching as well as a breastplate to prevent saddle slippage.

BEST JOB FOR THIS HORSE:
This horse can do anything if the saddle fits correctly, otherwise riding should be limited to level terrain and non-speed or non-jumping sports.

The area behind this horse's withers looks concave or hollowed out. It is a condition found in all breeds and can cause problems when the saddle isn't properly fitted.

Sometimes a hollowed back is rider induced by an individual who does not work the horse in collection or on the bit. Riding with incorrect contact can create a horse that is stiff and strung out behind. This condition is frequently seen in horses that do long-distance trail riding.

High Withers

DESCRIPTION:
The eighth through twelfth thoracic vertebrae are long and angle backward to create a steep, high withers.

HOW COMMON:
Common.

BREEDS/ACTIVITIES MOST AFFECTED:
Particularly Thoroughbreds, Saddlebreds, some Warmblood breeds. Affects any performance activity.

PERFORMANCE CONSEQUENCES:
• A high withers provides a lever for the muscles of the neck and back to work together in an efficient manner. As the horse's neck and head lower or extend, the back and loin muscles correspondingly shorten or lengthen. The backward angle of the withers is usually associated with a sloping shoulder which provides ample excursion of the shoulder blade. These features makes it very easy for a horse to engage in collection, to lengthen and round the back to clear jumping obstacles, and to extend the shoulders and back for improved stride length and speed. A horse with relatively high withers is capable of ease and efficiency of movement in any sport, making for a versatile equine athlete.
• If the withers are too high and narrow, there is a chance that a poorly fit saddle will impinge on the withers or slip back too far and create pain and discomfort to the horse particularly when the saddle compresses under a rider's weight. Performance and willingness to work will suffer in any sport. (See Hollow Behind Withers.)

MANAGEMENT/TRAINING STRATEGIES:
A saddle must be fit to the shape of the horse's withers. Consider that maturity and fitness will continue to improve breadth of muscular development to provide a better support for the saddle in this area. (See Hollow Behind Withers.)

BEST JOB FOR THIS HORSE:
Any athletic undertaking provided the horse wears a properly fit saddle.

A horse with high withers such as this can participate with ease in any sport, but proper saddle fit is critical.

This horse is beautifully rounded over the jump. High withers allow a horse to collect, engage his hind end, and round his back.

At Grand Prix level dressage horses are required to make flying lead changes with every stride. Such movements are easily performed by horses with features like high withers.

Roached Back

DESCRIPTION:
In the area where the back and loins join the croup, referred to as the coupling, there is an upward or convex curvature to the spine. This is often the result of a short back, or of injury to or malalignment of the lumbar vertebrae.

HOW COMMON:
Fairly common.

BREEDS/ACTIVITIES MOST AFFECTED:
Can affect any breed. Affects sports requiring collection such as dressage, stock horse, or jumping efforts.

PERFORMANCE CONSEQUENCES:
• A roached back is often accompanied by loin muscles that are less developed in substance, breadth, and strength. The spine is already "fixed" in a curved position and the attaching muscles are unable to contract appropriately to round and elevate the back. This makes it difficult for the horse to engage the haunches and round the back by elevating the muscles of the loins. The vertebrae often have reduced range of motion with the end result of the horse taking shorter steps behind. Jumping and dressage sports are particularly affected.
• These horses tend to be stiffer through the back and less flexible in both an up and down motion as well as bending side to side. There is back pain due to the vertebral impingement. This also makes for a less elastic feel beneath the rider as the back is more rigid. Agility sports like cutting, reining, barrel racing, gymkhana, and polo are more difficult for a horse with a rigid back.

MANAGEMENT/TRAINING STRATEGIES:
Suppling and stretching exercises for the back and strengthening of abdominal muscles aid these horses in achieving improved range of motion through the loins.

BEST JOB FOR THIS HORSE:
Trail riding, pleasure riding where no collection is required for long periods of time.

A horse with a roached or flat back may have limited flexibility in both an up-and-down motion as well as in bending from side-to-side.

When a horse rounds his back and engages his haunches he is using the muscles in his loins. In a horse with a roached back, these muscles may be less developed, affecting his ability to work in a discipline like dressage with skill.

A roached back is often a stiff one, making agility sports like cutting difficult for the horse.

Long or Weak Loins/Weak Coupling

DESCRIPTION:
Coupling describes the joining of the back to the croup at the lumbosacral (L-S) joint. Ideally the L-S joint should lie directly above the point of the hip. Weak coupling is often seen when the L-S joint is set further to the rear of the horse than the point of the hip. The loins are defined by the area of muscles formed by the last rib to the point of the hip. Normally, only two to three fingers' breadth should fit in this area. Loins are considered long if this span is more than a hand's breadth. Long loins are often associated with a long back. Often the croup is relatively flat and the quarters high.

HOW COMMON:
Common.

BREEDS/ACTIVITIES MOST AFFECTED:
Any breed may be affected. Affects all performance endeavors.

PERFORMANCE CONSEQUENCES:
• When a horse engages his hindquarters to collect, he does so by coiling the muscles of his loins and tensing his spinal column. A horse with weak or slack loins may be able to bend laterally quite well, but collection suffers since true collection depends on coiling of the loins to bend the hind leg joints. Because the hindquarters and hocks aren't able to be positioned beneath the horse's body, the hind legs string out behind, potentially throwing the horse more onto its forehand. This creates problems such as loss of coordination and balance as well as increased risk of forelimb lameness. To push off from the base of a jump or to negotiate a hill climb, a horse needs to be able to position its hind legs beneath its body to develop thrust. Downhill work requires a similar positioning of the rear limbs to serve as a brake. Weak loins inhibit this mechanical advantage, particularly affecting event horses, jumping horses, and trail horses.
• A horse's loins regulate the distribution of the weight on the forehand by enabling a horse to elevate its back and distribute the weight equally between front and rear ends. A horse that is unable to "coil" its loins moves with a stiff back and a flattened L-S joint, throwing the rear legs out behind like a marathon runner. Weak loins limit achievement of high performance in dressage. And, the lack of loin coiling affects reining, cutting, and polo horses to a degree as they are less able to explode with quick thrust when quickly changing direction.

MANAGEMENT/TRAINING STRATEGIES:
All efforts should be made to develop the haunches, the back, and abdominal muscles to improve efficiency of locomotion and to minimize muscular fatigue.

BEST JOB FOR THIS HORSE:
Pleasure equitation, pleasure riding, light trail riding.

Right: The area of muscles from a horse's last rib to the point of his hip is called the loins. If this area is more than a hand's width, a horse is considered long loined and probably long backed.

Below: When a horse jumps, coiling his loin muscles helps him to engage his hindquarters. For a sport like show jumping a horse needs very strong loin muscles to help him thrust and get up over a large obstacle.

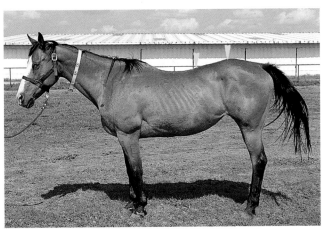

Above: A horse with weak loins may be able to move laterally quite well, but will have difficulty with quick bursts of speed, or quick stops.

Left: Weak loins can hamper a horse's ability to collect for the moves required in the higher levels of dressage.

Rough Coupling/Widow's Peak

DESCRIPTION:
In the region of the loins, the horse appears to have a hollow area considerably lower than the foremost part of the croup.

HOW COMMON:
Uncommon.

BREEDS/ACTIVITIES MOST AFFECTED:
Can affect any breed, but not much effect on performance.

PERFORMANCE CONSEQUENCES:
• A rough coupling is more cosmetically displeasing than functionally significant. Despite the horse appearing to have a low point in the loins in front of the croup, muscling of the loins may be ample and strong with minimal effect on the ability of the horse to collect its back or push with the haunches. However, a horse with poorly developed loin muscles will have difficulty in raising the center of the back for engagement of the hindquarters.

MANAGEMENT/TRAINING STRATEGIES:
Strengthening exercises for the back, abdominal muscles, and inner groin muscles make it easier for the horse to perform collected work.

BEST JOB FOR THIS HORSE:
Any sport provided adequate fitness is achieved.

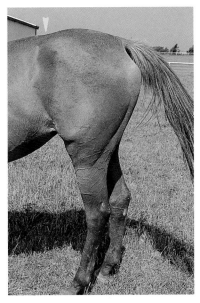

Left: The area in front of this horse's croup is concave and looks hollow. While it may be aesthetically displeasing, such conformation has little effect on performance.

Below Left: Exercises that strengthen his back, inner groin and abdominal muscles will make strong collection easier for the horse with rough coupling.

Photo by Nancy S. Loving, DVM

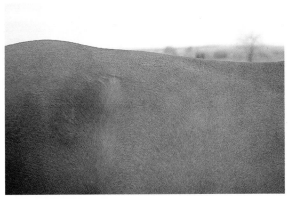

Above: A horse with rough coupling can perform in any sport with full range of motion.

Left: A horse's ability to work at collected gaits can be improved with exercises.

Hunter's Bump

DESCRIPTION:
Tearing of the ligaments at the sacroiliac (S-I) joint causes an enlargement at the top of the croup, or malalignment of the croup with the pelvis and lumbar vertebrae. One or both sides of the S-I joint may be affected.

HOW COMMON:
Fairly common.

BREEDS/ACTIVITIES MOST AFFECTED:
Most commonly seen in jumping horses.

PERFORMANCE CONSEQUENCES:
• This visible configuration to the croup is related to an injury incurred from excessive hindquarter effort in a horse that was unconditioned for the intended task, in a horse that may have had the hindquarters slip out beneath it, or in a horse that trotted a very steep hill. The injury usually heals with no other effects upon performance other than it being a weak point that could later be re-injured with subsequent strain of the ligaments. In cases of bony malalignment between the pelvis and the lumbar vertebrae, asymmetric movement of the hips may strain the lumbar back area as the horse's muscles attempt to compensate.
• A hunter's bump can develop on any horse, but is more often associated with a horse with a weak loin or long back that is unable to elevate the back or coil the loins appropriately for collection. It is commonly caused by overpacing young horses. Rider error that allows a horse to remain strung out at the base of a jump or the base of a steep hill also risks injury to this area of a horse's croup.

MANAGEMENT/TRAINING STRATEGIES:
Adequate conditioning of back, abdominal, and haunch muscles prevents strain as does rider skill at maintaining some degree of collection as a horse negotiates jumping obstacles. Caution in regulating speed is necessary when riding on slippery footing.

BEST JOB FOR THIS HORSE:
Anything once the injury has been addressed and allowed to fully heal.

Photos by Nancy S. Loving, DVM

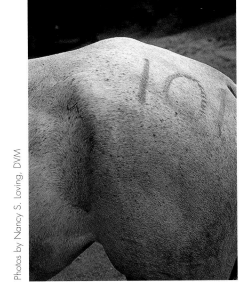

Above Left: Rather than being smoothly rounded, this horse's croup has a pronounced bump known as a Hunter's Bump. It is usually the result of torn ligaments.

Above Right: Trotting up a steep hill can cause injury to the sacroiliac joint and create a Hunter's Bump.

Center: Jumpers are most prone to Hunter's Bump since it is an injury that occurs when a horse is asked to thrust with his hind quarters as this horse is doing.

Left: The good news is that once a Hunter's Bump has healed it has little effect on a horse's performance.

Long Back

DESCRIPTION:

The back is measured from the peak of the withers to the peak of the croup. A back is considered long if it exceeds one-third of the horse's overall body length. A long back is often associated with long, weak loins.

HOW COMMON:

Common.

BREEDS/ACTIVITIES MOST AFFECTED:

Any breed, but a long back is often seen in Gaited horses, Saddlebreds, Thoroughbreds, and some Warmblood breeds. Any performance sport is affected.

PERFORMANCE CONSEQUENCES:

• The ability of a horse to engage in collection depends on well-developed back and abdominal muscles and the ability of the back to elevate, particularly in the area of the loins. A long back is flexible but makes it harder for a horse to stiffen and straighten the spine to develop speed, or to "coil" its loins to collect and engage the hindquarters to thrust the rear limbs forward. This directly affects work at the higher levels of dressage or agile movements of reining, cutting, barrel racing, and polo that rely on rapid engagement of the hindquarters to change direction and provide acceleration. Reduced flexion of a long back makes it difficult for the horse to round its back in a jumping bascule so it will be forced to jump in a flatter, less efficient frame.

• A long back is difficult to develop in muscle strength so is more likely to fatigue under the weight of a rider and may develop a sway over time. The abdominal muscles have greater difficulty compensating for the weak back and are less likely to develop with exercise. Loins and hindquarters may swing more than normal, increasing the occurrence of sore muscles of the lower back, which leads to a rigid, stiff ride. Cross-firing or speedy cutting are likely at high speeds. On the plus side, movement through a long back is flatter and quieter making for a more comfortable ride, and it is slightly easier for the horse to change its canter leads.

MANAGEMENT/TRAINING STRATEGIES:

Exercises should focus on developing fitness and strength through the back muscles, abdominal muscles, and haunch muscles. This can be accomplished with correct riding onto the bit to encourage collection; with cavalletti work, hill climbs on trails, and lateral work of half-pass, leg-yields, and serpentines; and with work on lunge line with side reins. Repeated transitions between trot and canter and canter and trot also develop these muscles.

BEST JOB FOR THIS HORSE:

Non-jumping sports and sports that do not depend on collection or extreme hind end use; pleasure riding, flat racing, light trail riding, lower levels of dressage.

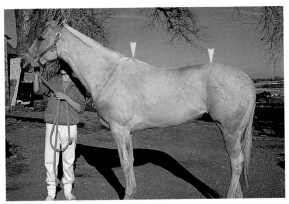

Left: A horse is considered long-backed if his back, as measured from withers to the peak of the croup, is more than 1/3 of his overall body length.

Below Left: The slide, a required move in reining, calls for a horse to rapidly engage his hindquarters and thrust the hind legs forward. Such a move may be hard for a horse with a long back.

Above: A long back can be strengthened with exercises that encourage collection, and work with the haunches such as hill climbing, lateral work at the half pass, leg yields, and serpentines.

Left: Cutting is another sport requiring extreme hind-end collection and sprinting. A long-backed horse is better suited to sports such as flat racing, pleasure riding, and dressage at the lower levels.

Short Back

DESCRIPTION:
A short back is one that measures less than one-third of the horse's overall length between the peak of the withers and the peak of the croup.

HOW COMMON:
Common.

BREEDS/ACTIVITIES MOST AFFECTED:
Any breed can be affected, although often seen in Quarter Horses, Arabians, and some Warmblood breeds.

PERFORMANCE CONSEQUENCES:
• A short back may lack flexibility and become stiff and rigid if proper measures are not taken to encourage suppleness and flexibility. If the vertebral spines of the back are excessively small, a horse may have difficulty bending and later develop spinal arthritis. This adversely affects performance at higher levels of dressage and jumping. When a horse is stiff or rigid in the back and torso, its stride will also be stiff and inelastic. The horse may over-reach, forge, or scalp if the hind legs move asynchronously from the front legs.
• On the plus side, a short-backed horse may be handy and agile, able to change direction quickly and with ease. This is favorable for reining, roping, cutting, and polo. And, a short-backed horse with good muscling is able to support the weight of a rider, with rare occurrences of back pain.

MANAGEMENT/TRAINING STRATEGIES:
Stretching exercises in a long and low frame increase suppleness in the back and neck to minimize stiffness. Lateral work and bending exercises improve flexibility through the loins and strength in the abdominal muscles.

BEST JOB FOR THIS HORSE:
Agility sports like reining, cutting, roping, trail riding.

Left Quarter horses, Arabians and Warmbloods are the breeds most likely to have short backs.

Below Left: A short back, one that is less than 1/3 of a horse's overall length, can be stiff and make collecting and bending harder for the horse.

Above: This obviously well-muscled and conditioned horse is well suited for the sport of roping. His short back helps him to make quick changes of direction.

Left: Barrel racing is an ideal sport for a horse with a short back since such conformation makes him quite agile and able to perform quick changes of direction.

Saddle-, Hollow-, or Low-Backed
Sway-Backed/Down in Back

DESCRIPTION:
The span of the back dips noticeably lower in the center of the back, forming a concave contour between the withers and the croup. This usually results in very high head carriage and stiffness through the neck. Often associated with a long back.

HOW COMMON: Fairly common.

BREEDS/ACTIVITIES MOST AFFECTED:
May occur in any breed horse. Affects all performance sports.

PERFORMANCE CONSEQUENCES:
• A sway back is often associated with weakness of the ligaments of the back due to multiple reasons:
　1. A broodmare that has had multiple foals often suffers loss of ligamentous strength and the back dips over time. 2. Old age in any horse is also accompanied by weakening of ligaments of the back. 3. Poor fitness and conditioning prevent adequate ligamentous support of back muscles. 4. Overuse injury to the muscles and ligaments occurs from excess work, excessive loads, or premature work on an immature horse. 5. In some cases, a straight back may appear swayed if it leads into a very high croup.
• A sway back often accompanies long loins. Because the loins are the least supported part of the back, they should be short and broad; if not, the ligamentous structures may weaken and the back drops. This positions a rider behind the horse's center of gravity to interfere with balance. And, a horse with a swayed back is unable to elevate the back to achieve collection. Any sport is affected, particularly dressage, jumping, stock work, and trail riding. The horse's back gets sore from its lack of supportive muscle strength and from the weight of the rider.
• A back with lax ligaments is unable to achieve rapid impulsion since the rear limbs have less connection with the front end of the horse. To achieve speed, the horse must be able to create some rigidity through the back and spine which a sway back precludes. This interferes with accomplishment in high-speed events such as racing, eventing, steeplechasing, timber racing, and polo.

MANAGEMENT/TRAINING STRATEGIES:
Minimal corrections can be made for a sway back since the ligaments are lax and unable to tighten. Exercises should be focused on abdominal and haunch muscular development. The horse should carry the lightest rider possible and be fitted with a comfortable saddle.

BEST JOB FOR THIS HORSE:
Pleasure riding only, teaching young students to ride.

The marked, concave contour of this horse's back between his withers and croup is called a sway back. Causes for this condition are many but it is most common in horses that are long-backed or long-loined.

Despite the rider's efforts, this horse is making a poor attempt at collecting. Collection occurs when a horse elevates his back, and long-loined horses often have weak muscles that make collection difficult.

A weak hind end makes it hard for a trail horse to trot uphill with his legs underneath him. Because of a low back, the horse may get sore when carrying anything but a light rider.

Short Croup

DESCRIPTION:
A short croup is often related to short quarters or a short pelvis. (Refer to Short Hindquarters for more detail.) The croup extends from the lumbosacral joint to the dock of the tail.

HOW COMMON:
Common.

BREEDS/ACTIVITIES MOST AFFECTED:
Quarter Horses, Arabians, Morgans, ponies, draft breeds.

PERFORMANCE CONSEQUENCES:
• A short croup often tends to be steep and angular. (Refer to Goose-Rumped for detail.) A shorter croup or pelvis provides less length of muscular attachments to the upper and lower thigh. This diminishes the horse's "engine" power in speed or jumping events. Keep in mind that a well-muscled croup may hide the structure of a short pelvis beneath.
• With a short croup, the lumbosacral joint is often located behind the point of the hips. A short croup is less effective as a muscular lever to achieve collection and to contract the abdominal underline of the horse as the back elevates and rounds. More muscular effort is required for a short-crouped horse to perform well in dressage or stock horse work.

MANAGEMENT/TRAINING STRATEGIES:
Lengthening and stretching exercises of the back and neck compensate for the reduced muscular efficiency in elevating the back of a horse with a short croup.

BEST JOB FOR THIS HORSE:
Pleasure riding, trail riding, driving in harness, non-speed or non-jumping events.

Left: A horse's croup is the area between the lumbosacral joint and the dock of the tail. A short croup frequently slopes downward at a steep angle as you can see here.

Below Left: A short croup is often accompanied by either short quarters or a short pelvis.

Above: Exercises that help to lengthen and strengthen the muscles of the back and abdomen can compensate for a short croup and help a horse achieve the pirouette or turn through the haunches seen here.

Left: Draft horses are commonly found to have short croups. Notice how this pair are pushing off their haunches and pulling with their shoulders.

Flat or Horizontal Croup

DESCRIPTION:
A flat croup is associated with a flat pelvis. The topline of the horse continues in a relatively flat manner all the way to the dock of the tail rather than falling off at an oblique angle over the hips. The ischium and sacrum of the pelvis point upward, with the rest of the pelvis structure also being long.

HOW COMMON:
Common.

BREEDS/ACTIVITIES MOST AFFECTED:
Arabians, Saddlebreds, Gaited horses.

PERFORMANCE CONSEQUENCES:
• A flat croup encourages a long, flowing stride and ground-covering trot because it allows the horse to push rearward with the hind legs with ease. This in turn helps the horse go faster, especially when the flat croup is sufficiently long to allow a greater range of muscle contraction to move the bony levers of the skeleton. Race horses do well with a croup angle of 25–30 degrees, while a trotting horse benefits from a slightly more oblique slope (35 degrees) to the croup. A driving horse that is not carrying weight suffers no ill effects in movement from having a flat croup. To prevent upward fixation of the patella, the horse endowed with a flat croup needs a long femur to create sufficient stifle angulation for locomotion.
• A flat croup makes it more difficult for a horse to engage the hindquarters so the back tends to stiffen. This makes it hard for a horse to achieve excellence in dressage or jumping work or in stock horse work. And, a flat croup minimizes the ability of a horse to develop power at slow paces as is necessary for draft horses.

MANAGEMENT/TRAINING STRATEGIES:
Back suppling and back and abdominal strengthening exercises are helpful to encourage a horse with this conformation to achieve some degree of collection.

BEST JOB FOR THIS HORSE:
Distance trail riding, showing, or carriage driving in harness.

Ideally the croup should slope gently towards the tail. This horse's topline is completely flat.

Flat croups are often found in Arabians and are responsible for this horse's long, flowing stride.

Horses with flat or horizontal croups cover ground well at the trot because they can easily push back with their hind legs. Distance trail riding is a suitable pursuit for such horses.

High Tail Set

DESCRIPTION:
A high tail carriage describes the appearance of the tail coming out of the body on a level with the top of the back.

HOW COMMON:
Common.

BREEDS/ACTIVITIES MOST AFFECTED:
Commonly seen in Arabians, Saddlebreds, Gaited horses, and Morgans.

PERFORMANCE CONSEQUENCE:
• A high tail set has no direct effect on performance consequences. It is often, but not always, associated with a flat croup; a high tail set contributes to the appearance of a horizontal croup which may be an aesthetic concern to some.

MANAGEMENT/TRAINING STRATEGIES:
There is nothing to be done to change the tail set of the horse as it directly relates to angle and length of the pelvis and sacrum. Training to relax the horse's mind in general will minimize the tendency to carry the tail flagged over the back.

BEST JOB FOR THIS HORSE:
A high tail set gives a horse an animated appearance which lends the horse well to showing, parade work, or driving in harness.

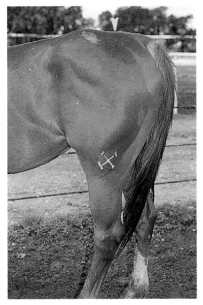

Left: This horse's tail begins at a point on top of his back rather than below it. This is considered a high tail set.

Below: Arabians often have high-set tails and carry them in this flaglike position when excited.

Above: While a high-set tail in no way affects a horse's performance, it gives the horse a more animated appearance.

Low Tail Set

DESCRIPTION:
A low tail set describes a tail that comes out of the body well down along the haunches. This is generally associated with a steep or goose-rumped pelvis.

HOW COMMON:
Common.

BREEDS/ACTIVITIES MOST AFFECTED:
Any breed, particularly draft horses, Quarter Horses.

PERFORMANCE CONSEQUENCES:
• The low tail set is only an aesthetic concern except as it is directly affected by the pelvic conformation. (For more detail refer to Goose-Rumped.)
• In the past, the low set of a tail of a draft horse caused concern that the tail might get caught in the traces or harness. This led to the practice of tail docking. Currently it is more acceptable to braid the tail and tie it up with elaborate ribbons rather than surgically removing a portion of the tail bone.

MANAGEMENT/TRAINING STRATEGIES:
There is nothing to be done to change the tail set of the horse as it directly relates to angle and length of the pelvis and sacrum.

BEST JOB FOR THIS HORSE:
Anything appropriate to a horse with a steep pelvis, particularly power required at slow paces.

A low tail is one that comes out of the horse's body well down the haunches. Such conformation is usually indicative of a steep pelvis.

Quarter horses and draft horses frequently have tails that are set low.

This horse has both a low-set tail and a steep croup. While the low-set tail does not affect its ability to perform, its steep croup may make the strong collection needed in dressage difficult.

Wry Tail/Tail Carried to One Side

DESCRIPTION:
The horse carries the tail cocked to one side rather than the tail falling in a line parallel to the spine.

HOW COMMON:
Common.

BREEDS/ACTIVITIES MOST AFFECTED:
Arabians.

PERFORMANCE CONSEQUENCES:
• The tail may be carried to the side if the horse is not perfectly straight between the rider's aids. Like a rudder, the horse uses its tail as a balancing pole. This is useful to determine how straight a horse is traveling behind, and whether or not the horse is falling more onto one shoulder than another. Over time, incorrect body carriage may place undue stress on one or more limbs and lead to lameness.
• A horse may move with its tail cocked for reasons related to injury or discomfort, using the tail as a "brace." Watch the horse's pelvic swing to see if it is locked and rigid, indicating pain in the rear legs or back.

MANAGEMENT/TRAINING STRATEGIES:
Training the horse to move straight between hand and leg aids often eliminates the crooked tail carriage. Have a thorough veterinary exam to rule out pain or discomfort in the rear legs or back. And, check that the horse's tail hasn't been injured or broken some time in the past.

BEST JOB FOR THIS HORSE:
Anything provided the horse learns to move straight beneath the rider.

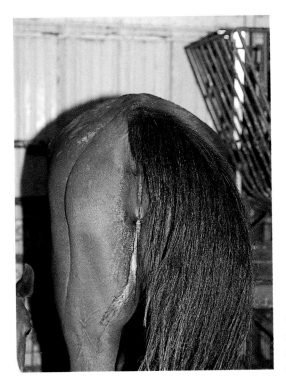

When a horse carries its tail to one side it may be because the animal is not straight between the rider's aids, or it may be because of an injury.

Wide Chest/Barrel Rib Cage

DESCRIPTION:
Rounded ribs increase the dimensions of the chest, giving a rounded, cylindrical or barrel shape to the rib cage. The length of the ribs tends to be short.

HOW COMMON:
Common.

BREEDS/ACTIVITIES MOST AFFECTED:
Can affect any breed, but commonly seen in Quarter Horses or Warmblood breeds.

PERFORMANCE CONSEQUENCES:
• A barrel rib cage provides ample expansion for the lungs and inspiratory muscles, but too much roundness increases the size of the horse's barrel (or chest) and may restrict upper arm movement, length of stride, and speed. Round ribs coupled with short rib length further restrict the length and reach of the shoulder.
• A rounded rib cage pushes a rider's legs further to the side of his or her body, stretching the ligaments and joints of the pelvis and hips. This can be very uncomfortable for the rider, particularly in sports that require a long time in the saddle, such as hunting, trail riding, and ranch work. Sports that require sensitive leg aids such as dressage, cutting, and reining may also increase stress on the rider's pelvic structures on an especially wide-barreled horse.

MANAGEMENT/TRAINING STRATEGIES:
Fit the horse with a close contact saddle to further reduce the physical spread of the rider's pelvis. Keep the horse in excellent body condition, not too fat and not too lean, to also prevent pelvic spread for the rider and to maximize fluid movement of the horse's shoulders and arms.

BEST JOB FOR THIS HORSE:
Anything is possible coupled with good conditioning and fitness.

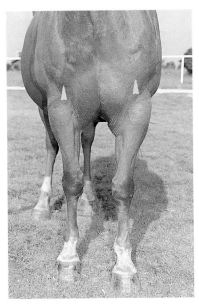

While a wide chest means a lot of room for a horse to expand his lungs, one that is too wide can restrict his stride-length and speed.

A barrel rib cage can mean an uncomfortable ride. Notice how this rider's legs are pushed out away from her horse's sides. On long rides her pelvis and hips may get sore.

Pear-Shaped Ribcage/Widens Toward Flanks

DESCRIPTION:
A pear-shaped ribcage tends to be narrow at the girth and behind the girth at mid-chest, then widens toward the flanks.

HOW COMMON:
Common.

BREEDS/ACTIVITIES MOST AFFECTED:
Arabians, Saddlebreds, Gaited horses.

PERFORMANCE CONSEQUENCES:
• A pear-shaped ribcage makes it difficult to hold a saddle in place on the horse's back without use of a breast collar or crupper, particularly when riding over uneven terrain, in jumping pursuits, or low crouching work and quick direction changes as seen with reining, cutting, and polo. When the saddle continually shifts, the rider's balance on the horse's back is affected, forcing both horse and rider to constantly make adjustments. This leads to muscle fatigue of both horse and rider. The saddle slippage has the potential to create friction and rub spots on the horse's back and may lead to sore back muscles.
• The narrowness of the chest just behind the girth makes leg aid contact challenging, just as with a slab-sided horse.

MANAGEMENT/TRAINING STRATEGIES:
Find a saddle that remains as stable as possible in the center of the back, and use a breast collar and crupper as necessary.

BEST JOB FOR THIS HORSE:
Riding pursuits on level terrain to minimize saddle movement. Non-jumping activities.

Photo by Nancy S. Loving, DVM

This horse has a pear-shaped ribcage, meaning that it is narrow at the girth and widens toward the flanks. This makes it hard to hold a saddle in place, and a crupper or breast collar is needed.

Well-Sprung Ribs

DESCRIPTION:
Well-sprung ribs angle backward with sufficient length, breadth, and spacing to provide an arched rib cage and chest with deep dimensions from front of the chest to the back. The largest part of the barrel sits just behind the girth. The last rib is sprung outward and inclined to the rear, with the other ribs conforming similarly in length, roundness of contour, and rearward directed angle.

HOW COMMON:
Common.

BREEDS/ACTIVITIES MOST AFFECTED:
Any breed. Favorable for any sport.

PERFORMANCE CONSEQUENCES:
• Well-sprung ribs promote strong breathing and air intake. This improves a horse's performance capacity related to efficiency of muscular metabolism.
• Well-sprung ribs provide an ample area of attachment of shoulder, leg, and neck muscles to the body, enabling a large range of motion for muscular contraction for length and speed of stride. A rider's weight is easily balanced and stabilized within the center of the horse's back since the saddle stays steady and the girth holds its position. The ample rib length associated with this preferred conformational characteristic is proportional to the size and width of the vertebrae which influence the breadth and strength of attaching muscles in the back and loins. With a well-sprung rib conformation, there is sufficient room for development of strong loin muscles while still maintaining a short loin distance between the last rib and the point of the hip, referred to as close coupling.

MANAGEMENT/TRAINING STRATEGIES:
Conditioning and fitness training take advantage of the horse's inherent athletic capabilities.

BEST JOB FOR THIS HORSE:
Anything, especially speed and jumping activities that require huge muscular efforts and lots of air intake.

Above: The widest point on this horse's barrel is just behind the girth. Such a horse is well-suited to any discipline.

Right: Well-sprung ribs give ample room for breathing and air intake. Such a horse is ideal for speed sports.

Above: Because of the slope of this horse's barrel, the rider is able to maintain close contact with her leg over the jump.

Slab-Sided

DESCRIPTION:
A slab-sided horse has poor spring of the ribs due to flatness and vertical alignment of the ribs although the ribs are adequate in length.

HOW COMMON:
Common.

BREEDS/ACTIVITIES MOST AFFECTED:
Thoroughbreds, Saddlebreds, Tennessee Walking horses, Gaited horses.

PERFORMANCE CONSEQUENCES:
• The chest of a slab-sided horse has less room for the lungs to expand. This may limit efficiency of muscular metabolism with arduous and prolonged exercise.
• In a horse with short depth of chest limited lung capacity is likely to limit the ability for speed work.
• Although a lengthy rib cage imparts lateral flexibility, the narrowness of a slab-sided horse makes it difficult for a rider to apply leg aids since the rider's legs often hang down without fully closing around the horse's body. It is also more of an effort to balance on the horse's back because of limited leg contact, and because the saddle tends to shift side to side. The horse also has a harder time carrying the rider's weight because of a reduced base of support by relatively narrow back muscles.

MANAGEMENT/TRAINING STRATEGIES:
Enhance a horse's sensitivity to leg aids, seat aids, and hand aids so minimal efforts are needed by the rider to affect movement and change in direction. Fit the saddle well to the contours of the horse's back, providing sufficient padding over narrow back muscles. Use a breast collar or crupper as needed. Strengthen back and abdominal muscles with hill work, trotting cavallettis, jumping grids, lateral and collected work of half-pass, leg-yield, serpentines, and spiraling in and out on circles. Also incorporate upward and downward transitions between trot and canter, and halt and canter.

BEST JOB FOR THIS HORSE:
Any sport is appropriate provided the rider has a balanced seat, the saddle fits the horse well, and the horse is fit for the intended task.

Left: A slab-sided horse has long ribs but they are flat rather than gently rounded.

Below Left: Because this horse's sides are so narrow, it is not difficult for the rider to get his legs down and around the horse.

Above: Lateral movements aren't difficult for the slab-sided horse but notice how far back the rider's leg has slipped.

Left: A slab-sided horse should be able to work at any discipline when properly trained, but his lung capacity may be limited because of his narrow build.

Tucked Up/Herring-Gutted/Wasp-Waisted

DESCRIPTION:
The appearance of the waist beneath the flanks is angular, narrow, and tucked up with limited development of the abdominal muscles. This is often associated with short rear ribs. (Undernourished horses would also exhibit prominent ribs and little or no fat at the withers, neck, and tailbase.)

HOW COMMON:
Common.

BREEDS/ACTIVITIES MOST AFFECTED:
Can affect any breed. Affects all performance activities, particularly dressage, jumping, eventing, cutting, reining, roping, and gymkhana.

PERFORMANCE CONSEQUENCES:
• A wasp-waisted appearance is often the result of how a horse is trained and ridden. Horses that do not use their backs and don't engage the haunches in a collected or semi-collected frame never fully develop their abdominal musculature. These horses appear to be "lean, mean, running machines," like a greyhound, with stringy muscles along the topline and gaskins as well.
• The lack of abdominal development reduces the overall strength of a horse's movement. Stamina is reduced, and the back is predisposed to injury. The horse is incapable of moving in a fluid, elastic stride although it is probably quite capable of covering ground despite the lack of correct body carriage.

MANAGEMENT/TRAINING STRATEGIES:
Training the horse to accept bit contact, to elevate the back and engage the haunches will begin to develop the underline and abdominal muscles to encourage overall strength. Over time the underline will become more parallel to the ground, and all the muscles should lose their stringy appearance.

BEST JOB FOR THIS HORSE:
Speed and jumping sports should be avoided until the horse develops better strength and tone of both the top and underline muscles.

Left: A horse can appear wasp-waisted when his abdominal muscles have not been properly conditioned. The area beneath this horse's flanks looks pinched and narrow.

Below: This horse's trot is loose and he will likely tire more easily than a horse that has been well developed.

When a horse isn't trained to collect and use his back and hind end, his abdominal muscles don't get properly worked. This horse's abdominals show no development.

Depth of Back

DESCRIPTION:
The vertical distance from the lowest point of the horse's back to the bottom of the abdomen. This point in front of the sheath or udder should be parallel to the ground and comparable in depth to the front portion of the chest just behind the elbow at the girth.

HOW COMMON:
Common.

BREEDS/ACTIVITIES MOST AFFECTED:
Any breed, especially Warmblood breeds, Quarter Horses, and Morgans. Favorably affects all sports.

PERFORMANCE CONSEQUENCES:
• Good depth to the back indicates a horse with strong abdominal musculature development important for strength and speed. This configuration is critical to excellence in dressage, jumping, and racing pursuits. Strong abdominal muscles go hand-in-hand with a strong, effective back that is suited for carrying a rider's weight and for engaging the haunches to initiate thrust for acceleration, speed, and jumping, or for collected work.
• Depth of back is not to be confused with an obese horse kept in "show" condition, as fat only conceals a tendency to be wasp-waisted due to short last ribs while doing nothing for functional efficiency in locomotion.

MANAGEMENT/TRAINING STRATEGIES:
Capitalize on the inherent strength of this horse's structure by developing conditioning and fitness.

BEST JOB FOR THIS HORSE:
This horse can perform anything provided it is conditioned to the task.

The depth of a horse's back is measured from the lowest point of his back to the bottom of his abdomen. This distance should be the same as the depth of the front of his chest, measured at the girth.

A horse with good depth of back usually has strong abdominal muscles, an attribute critical for top level dressage.

The spin that is practiced in reining calls for strong haunches and strong abdominal muscles. Both can be well developed in a horse with good depth of back.

Conformation and Performance

Front Legs

Straight, Upright, or Vertical Shoulder

DESCRIPTION:
The direction of the shoulder blade as measured from the top of the withers to the point of the shoulder lies in an upright position, particularly as it follows the scapular spine. Often accompanies low withers.

HOW COMMON:
Common.

BREEDS/ACTIVITIES MOST AFFECTED:
Any breed may be affected, especially Quarter Horses. Affects all sports.

PERFORMANCE CONSEQUENCES:
• An upright shoulder has shorter muscular attachments that have less ability to contract and lengthen than seen with a sloping shoulder. The horse's stride length is shortened, requiring an increased number of footsteps to cover the ground. This means a greater risk of injury to structures of the front legs and hastened onset of fatigue.
• A relatively vertical shoulder imparts a rough, inelastic ride due to high knee action and short steps, with the rider's back feeling the jar of each limb strike. This increases concussion on the front limbs with the possibility of developing degenerative joint disease (DJD) or navicular problems in a hard-working athlete. The stress of impact tends to stiffen and tighten the shoulder muscles, making the horse less supple with reduced range of motion that normally imparts a long stride reach.
• A steep, upright shoulder causes the shoulder joint to be open and set low over a short, steep arm bone, making it more difficult for a horse to elevate the shoulders and close the angles in a tight fold, so important for jumping or cutting type activities. However, this configuration makes it easier for a horse to accelerate quickly in sprinting activities.

MANAGEMENT/TRAINING STRATEGIES:
Stretching exercises that improve back flexibility and strength will lessen work effort by the front limbs and reduce fatigue, while additionally improving elasticity of the gaits to give a somewhat less jarring ride.

BEST JOB FOR THIS HORSE:
Gaiting or park showing; parade horse; sprint activities like roping or Quarter Horse racing.

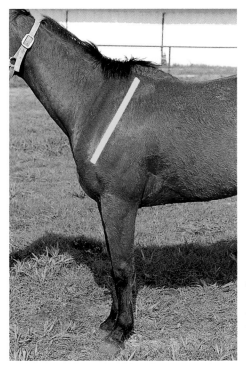

A straight-shouldered horse tends to move with short, choppy strides that can be uncomfortable for the rider and tiring for the horse.

An upright shoulder has shorter muscle attachments than a sloping shoulder and this in turn limits the horse's ability to extend his stride.

Laid-Back or Sloping Shoulder

DESCRIPTION:
This describes an oblique angle of the shoulder as measured from the top of the withers to the point of the shoulder, with the withers set well behind the elbow. Often accompanies a deep chest and moderately high withers.

HOW COMMON:
Common.

BREEDS/ACTIVITIES MOST AFFECTED:
Jumping, racing, cutting, reining, polo, eventing, and dressage.

PERFORMANCE CONSEQUENCES:
• A sloping shoulder is a long shoulder blade to which attaching muscles effectively contract to increase extension and efficiency of the stride. The long slope of the shoulder distributes muscular attachments of the shoulder to the body over a large area. This decreases the jar of the ride and prevents stiffening of the horse's shoulders with impact. A laid-back shoulder imparts elasticity and freedom of swing through the shoulders enabling a horse to take fluid, extended strides to cover ground or to display athletic ease of effort in sports like dressage or jumping. An efficient stride and long reach contribute to stamina and assist in maintaining speed. (Refer to Short Neck for more detail.)
• The longer the bones of the shoulder blade and arm bone, the more advantageous the shoulder angle to improve the horse's ability to fold the front legs in a tight tuck over fences. A laid-back scapula slides back towards the horizontal as the horse lifts its front legs to increase the horse's "scope." Such a mobile shoulder imparts good shock-absorption properties important to a jumping horse. At the same time it provides a comfortable ride because the slope to the shoulder sets the withers back so the rider is not seated over the front legs but instead is positioned in the "spring" of the horse's back.

MANAGEMENT/TRAINING STRATEGIES:
Proper conditioning of the back, loins, and abdominal muscles builds muscular strength and fitness to enable the horse to achieve inherent gait extension and a fluid shoulder swing.

BEST JOB FOR THIS HORSE:
Jumping, cutting, dressage, eventing, racing (flat, harness, or endurance), polo, or driving in harness.

Right: A longer, sloping shoulder such as this allows a horse to take longer, more fluid strides.

Below: A good jumper is able to tightly tuck his knees up over a fence. Longer shoulder blades and arm bones help him to do this.

Above: Because of the elasticity of his front end this cutting horse has no difficulty crouching down. He is helped by his long sloping shoulders.

Above: The slope of the shoulders helps the rider to sit back over this horse's center of balance and not on his front end. This is critical in sports, like polo, with its quick changes of direction.

Long Arm Bone (Humerus)

DESCRIPTION:
The arm bone extends between the point of the shoulder to the elbow, and its length dictates how tightly the elbow and lower joints can bend and how long the leg reaches in extension. The arm bone is considered long when it is 50–60 percent of the length of the scapula. The elbow is situated beneath the middle of the withers in a horse with a long arm bone.

HOW COMMON:
Common.

BREEDS/ACTIVITIES MOST AFFECTED:
Jumping, steeplechase, eventing, lateral movements of dressage, and cutting.

PERFORMANCE CONSEQUENCES:
• A long arm bone increases the movement of the elbow away from the horse's torso both forward and to the side, enabling greater "scope" accomplished with tightly tucked limbs over a fence or increased stride length in speed events.
• A long arm bone provides a scaffold for lengthy muscle attachments (of flexor and extensor muscles) which contract with greater force to give a horse more power and speed.

MANAGEMENT/TRAINING STRATEGIES:
To further improve a horse's scope, work on exercises to strengthen the back and loins to assist engagement of the hindquarters to help elevate the front quarters over jumps, in low crouching positions of cutting or reining, and in collected work of dressage.

BEST JOB FOR THIS HORSE:
Speed events, jumping, and dressage.

Left: A horse's arm bone is measured from the point of the shoulder to the elbow. A longer arm bone means greater stride length and extension both necessary for top level dressage work.

Left: Notice how much this race horse is able to extend his front leg. A long arm bone provides for longer flexor and extensor muscles which when contracted give a horse increased speed and power.

Far Left: Long arm bones mean greater scope in a horse allowing him to tightly tuck his knees as this jumper is doing.

Left: A half pass and lateral movements in general are easier for a horse that has long arm bones.

Short Arm Bone (Humerus)

DESCRIPTION:
A short arm bone connecting the shoulder joint with the elbow is usually oriented in a horizontal position and in so doing closes the shoulder angle to less than 90 degrees.

HOW COMMON:
Common.

BREEDS/ACTIVITIES MOST AFFECTED:
Quarter Horses, Paint horses, Warmbloods.

PERFORMANCE CONSEQUENCES:
• A short humerus decreases the "scope" of the horse, and contributes to a short, choppy stride. The horse is also less able to execute lateral movements common in dressage and cutting. However, a horizontal arm bone is advantageous for forward propulsion important to sprinting sports.
• The pony-gaited stride created by a short arm bone contributes to increased impact stress on the front limbs and especially the feet. Not only does the rider feel jarred by the motion, but the horse also absorbs a lot of concussion in its legs. Many steps are needed to cover the ground, increasing the chance to develop front end lameness problems.

MANAGEMENT/TRAINING STRATEGIES:
Develop strength and handiness of forearm muscles by exercising in hill climbs and descents, trotting cavallettis and jumping grids, and in lateral work of leg-yield, half-pass, spiraling in and out of circles. Shoe the horse with adequate caudal heel support of the front feet and with shock-absorbing shoes or pads to minimize concussion trauma to the navicular structures and lower joints.

BEST JOB FOR THIS HORSE:
Pleasure riding; non-impact activities; sprinting sports like roping or barrel racing.

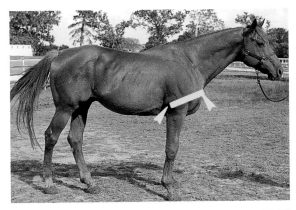

A short arm bone usually connects the elbow and shoulder joint horizontally. This limits range of motion for the horse and is most common in Quarter horses, Warmbloods and Paints.

This horse has a very short stride because of a short arm bone. Lateral motions and scope are most affected by this conformation, and speed will be limited.

This horse will never be a top quality jumper because of the way he carries his knees. Short arm bones limit him in tucking his knees up tightly over the fence as is desired.

Narrow Breast

DESCRIPTION:
With the horse squared up and viewed from the front, the width between the front legs is relatively narrow. Note that breast width varies depending on how wide apart the feet are placed at rest. Width of the breast often represents the general thickness and development of the shoulders.

HOW COMMON:
Fairly common.

BREEDS/ACTIVITIES MOST AFFECTED:
Gaited horses, Saddlebreds, Paso Finos, Tennessee Walking horses.

PERFORMANCE CONSEQUENCES:
• The ability of a horse to carry weight is often correlated to the width of the breast, so a narrow-breasted horse would not do well with draft work but may perform adequately in harness or carrying a light rider. The narrowness of the breast may result from turned-in elbows that also causes the toes to turn out. (Refer to Base Wide, Toed-Out.)
• A narrow breast may be the result of immaturity, poor body condition or emaciation from inadequate nutrition, or as a result of under-developed breast muscles due to prolonged idle time in the pasture and a lack of consistent work and development of fitness. Often a narrow-breasted horse also has undeveloped neck and shoulder muscles.
• A narrow-breasted horse often tends to "plait," and as the legs come into close contact, the horse is more likely to interfere (anywhere from the knees to the coronary band) with the opposite foreleg, especially at trot or pace.

MANAGEMENT/TRAINING STRATEGIES:
General conditioning aids development of the pectoral muscles. Hill work, particularly steep descents, use breast muscles as brakes for movement of the horse's mass down a hill. Cavalletti work at the trot also strengthens breast and shoulder muscles as the horse actively picks up the front legs. Lateral work of dressage strengthens and develops the breast, shoulder, and medial forearm muscles. Use of lower leg boots is wise to protect against interference injury.

BEST JOB FOR THIS HORSE:
Pleasure riding; driving in harness; light trail riding.

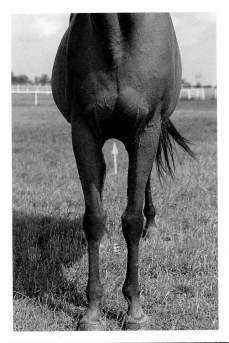

A narrow breasted horse will not be as strong as a wide breasted one. While some horses are born this way, others are narrow through lack of work or poor nutrition.

Gaited horses, Saddlebreds, Paso Finos and Tennessee Walking horses are most likely to be narrow breasted.

Pigeon-Breasted

DESCRIPTION:
The front legs are set too far back beneath the body, giving a bulky appearance to the breast as viewed from the side suggestive of the protrusive breast of a pigeon. Because of this conformation, the horse's fore feet land behind a line drawn from the withers to the ground, setting him back under himself. A pigeon breast is often associated with a long shoulder blade which drops the point of the shoulder somewhat low with the arm bone oriented relatively horizontal; this sets the elbows more to the rear of the horse.

HOW COMMON:
Uncommon.

BREEDS/ACTIVITIES MOST AFFECTED:
Quarter Horses with big bulky muscles.

PERFORMANCE CONSEQUENCES:
• The bulky muscles of the breast and the movement of the front feet beneath the horse decrease the efficiency of the stride, limit the swing of the shoulders, and generally hasten fatigue. These features are amplified by a breast that is also too wide; its breadth interferes with excursion of the front limbs forcing them to move to the side rather than directly beneath the horse. The "rolling" gait that results slows speed, particularly at a gallop.
• The position of the front legs should have little interference with sprinting sports that depend upon rapid acceleration from the start box, like Quarter Horse racing, barrel racing, or roping. In fact, the inverted V of the pectoral muscles is important to the quick turns, dodges, and spins favored by stock work like cutting and reining.

MANAGEMENT/TRAINING STRATEGIES:
Good conditioning strategies to improve muscular and cardiovascular fitness to minimize muscular fatigue.

BEST JOB FOR THIS HORSE:
Sprint sports such as Quarter Horse racing, barrel racing, or roping; stock horse sports that require low front end crouches, quick turns, or sliding stops.

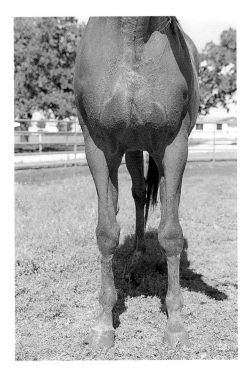

This horse's legs are set far back beneath him giving his chest a meaty or pigeon-breasted appearance.

Legs set back under the body are an advantage for sports like cutting and roping that require rapid acceleration and quick changes of direction.

Long Forearm

DESCRIPTION:
The length of the radius between the elbow and the carpus is long.

HOW COMMON:
Common.

BREEDS/ACTIVITIES MOST AFFECTED:
Affects all breeds, especially Thoroughbreds, Saddlebreds, Tennessee Walking horses, Arabians, and Warmblood horses. Affects all sports activities.

PERFORMANCE CONSEQUENCES:
• A long forearm is desirable to any performance activity, especially when coupled with a short cannon bone. Length to the radius increases the surface area and length of muscular attachments to gain the greatest biomechanical leverage to impart speed and maximize stride length. These qualities are critical to a racehorse, eventer, steeplechaser, timber chaser, harness racer, endurance horse, to name a few.
• Good muscling of a long forearm is particularly advantageous to horses involved in jumping activities as the strong forearm muscles absorb concussion from impact and at the same time diffuse strain on the tendons and joints upon landing.

MANAGEMENT/TRAINING STRATEGIES:
Maximize the horse's fitness and condition to take advantage of this inherent structural attribute.

BEST JOB FOR THIS HORSE:
Speed events, jumping events, long-distance trail riding.

Long forearms will affect the performance of any breed and could be especially advantageous to jumpers if accompanied by good muscling.

Long forearms mean longer muscles with greater surface area. These factors translate to a potential for increased speed and longer stride length, critical to horses engaged in racing and endurance activities.

Short Forearm

DESCRIPTION:
The distance of the radius between the elbow and the carpus is proportionately short.

HOW COMMON:
Uncommon.

BREEDS/ACTIVITIES MOST AFFECTED:
Quarter Horses, Morgans. Affects speed and jumping events.

PERFORMANCE CONSEQUENCES:
• Because the length of a horse's stride is quite dependent on a lengthy forearm in addition to a sloping shoulder, a short forearm causes a horse to necessarily increase the number of steps to cover a certain distance as compared to a horse with a long forearm. More steps taken increases the overall muscular effort and hastens the onset of fatigue.
• A short forearm increases the action of the knees, giving the horse an animated appearance that is desirable for a parade horse, show horse, or carriage horse. Greater knee action is not compatible with speed.

MANAGEMENT/TRAINING STRATEGIES:
Conditioning and fitness make this horse's work easier despite the increased number of steps needed to cover ground. Diligent attention should be paid to level trimming with adequate shoe support of the caudal foot, as increased concussion and impact on the lower legs from high action increases the risk of career-threatening lameness.

BEST JOB FOR THIS HORSE:
Showing, hunter equitation, driving in harness, parade work; minimal effect on stock horse sprint activities like cutting, reining, roping, and barrel racing.

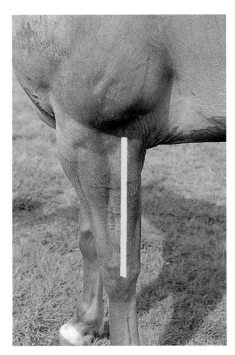

Short forearms result in a shorter stride and therefore more steps to cover the same ground. Fatigue is a possibility in a horse with this structure because of the relatively greater muscular effort.

A horse with short forearms works well in harness where speed and long strides are not critical.

Long Cannon Bone

DESCRIPTION:
The cannon bone is long between the knee and the fetlock making the knees appear high relative to the overall balance of the horse.

HOW COMMON:
Common

BREEDS/ACTIVITIES MOST AFFECTED:
Trail riding, long-distance events like eventing, endurance, combined driving, and polo.

PERFORMANCE CONSEQUENCES:
• Long cannons reduce the mechanical advantage of the muscular pull of the tendons on the lower leg. Uneven terrain or unlevel foot balance will magnify stress on the carpus above since the lengthy tendons associated with a long cannon are not as stabilizing to the lower limb.
• Long cannon bones increase the weight on the end of the limb, contributing to a less efficient and less stable movement. Added weight to the front legs increases the muscular effort involved in picking up the limbs, leading to hastened fatigue.
• There is a greatly increased risk of tendon/ligament injury, especially when the horse is also tied-in at the knee.

MANAGEMENT/TRAINING STRATEGIES:
Fitness and conditioning are all important in maximizing a horse's mechanical efficiency to minimize the effort of work. Hill climbing increases muscular strength, while gymnastic grids improve coordination and muscular development particularly of the back, haunch, and abdominal muscles. Shoe with adequate support to the rear of the front feet to improve stability of front limbs.

BEST JOB FOR THIS HORSE:
Flat racing short distances.

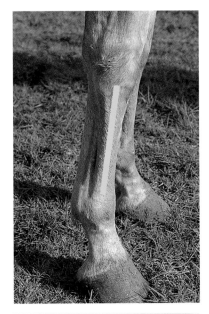

Left: The cannon bone is one of the most critical to a horse. Because horses carry more weight on their front legs than their back ones, the front cannon bone that is long—and its associated tendons and ligaments—take a lot of the stress when the horse moves.

Above: A horse's cannon bone is said to be long when the knees appear to be high as compared to the overall balance of the horse.

Left: Working through deep footing like sand, a horse with long cannon bones will likely get tired more quickly than one with short cannon bones, because he is carrying more weight on his front end and the muscular pull of the tendons is less efficient.

Left: Working on uneven terrain such as this puts added stress on the lengthy tendons associated with long cannon bones.

Photo by Nancy S. Loving, DVM

Short Cannon Bone

DESCRIPTION:
The cannon bone is short relative to the forearm bone (radius). This is a desirable characteristic of any performance horse.

HOW COMMON:
Common.

BREEDS/ACTIVITIES MOST AFFECTED:
Any breed and any sport.

PERFORMANCE CONSEQUENCES:
• If you think of the carpus or the hock as the pulley over which tendons pass, and the muscles of a long forearm or the gaskin as levers, then you can see that a short lever arm (cannon bone) on the end of the pulley improves the ease and power of force generated by the muscles of a long forearm or gaskin. This enables an efficient pull of the tendons across the back of the knee or the point of the hock to move the limb forward and back.
• A relatively short cannon bone as compared to the forearm bone also reduces the weight of the lower leg so that less muscular effort is needed to move the limb. Such mechanical efficiency contributes to speed, stamina, soundness, and jumping ability.

MANAGEMENT/TRAINING STRATEGIES:
To take advantage of the mechanical efficiency created by a short cannon, condition the horse's cardiovascular and musculoskeletal system over months and years to maximize athletic longevity.

BEST JOB FOR THIS HORSE:
Anything, from low-impact to high-impact sports, from low-speed to high-speed sports assuming no other glaring conformational defects exist.

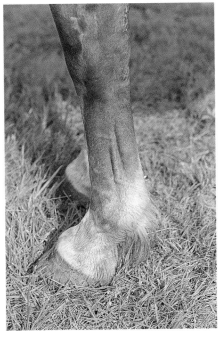

Photo by Nancy S. Loving, DVM

Photo by Nancy S. Loving, DVM

Above Left: Horses with short cannon bones may participate in both low and high impact sports, as well as low and high speed sports.

Above Right: Ideally you want a horse with a short cannon bone like this, coupled with a long forearm.

Center: With a short cannon bone, there is less weight on the lower leg and less muscle is needed to lift it. Consequently a horse will tire less easily, especially important for trail or endurance horses.

Left: Short cannon bones make for efficient use of the front end as is necessary in sports like reining.

Insufficient Bone

DESCRIPTION:
Measurement of the circumference of the top of the cannon bone just beneath the knee joints gives an estimation of bone substance. Ideally, a 1,000-pound horse should have a circumference of 7–8 inches to be considered adequate. A horse with insufficient bone has less than 7 inches in circumference for every 1,000 pounds of body weight.

HOW COMMON:
Fairly common.

BREEDS/ACTIVITIES MOST AFFECTED:
Speed events, jumping, or distance sports.

PERFORMANCE CONSEQUENCES:
• Muscles are only as strong as the bones to which they attach. A horse with insufficient bone structure, particularly in relation to its body mass, is more at risk of injury. Injury is incurred within the joints, muscles, tendons, ligaments, feet, or within the bones themselves.
• Repeated impact to the limbs of a horse with insufficient bone potentially creates soundness issues, particularly in sports that stimulate a lot of concussion such as jumping, galloping, racing, or prolonged periods of trail riding. Track horses experience bucked shins, while event horses and trail horses experience strained tendons and ligaments from sustained activity on inadequate bone structure. Horses that have large, heavy bones are less prone to lameness, at least with speed work, than lighter individuals.

MANAGEMENT/TRAINING STRATEGIES:
Fitness and conditioning are critical to develop strong muscling, but concussion sports as noted should be avoided if your horse is to maintain athletic longevity. Adequate vitamin and mineral intake while growing will enable bones to develop strength when combined with an appropriate training schedule.

BEST JOB FOR THIS HORSE:
Equitation classes, harness work at moderate speeds, pleasure riding.

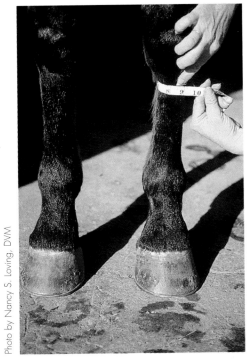

Photo by Nancy S. Loving, DVM

You can estimate a horse's bone substance by measuring the circumference of the top of the cannon bone just above his knee. A 1,000-pound horse should measure 7 to 8 inches around the cannon bone. Strong bones mean strong muscles and tendons.

A horse with thin bones is much more prone to injury, and repeated impact to limbs that are thin-boned may create soundness problems.

Tied-in Below the Knee

DESCRIPTION:
The back of the cannon just below the knee appears "cut out" with decreased tendon diameter at this point. Rather than the cannon bone and flexor tendons having the preferred parallel alignment when viewed in profile, the circumference at the top of the tendons is narrower than the circumference measured just above the fetlock.

HOW COMMON:
Common.

BREEDS/ACTIVITIES MOST AFFECTED:
Speed events such as racing and polo, and concussion athletics such as jumping, steeplechase, endurance, eventing.

PERFORMANCE CONSEQUENCES:
• The narrow tendon diameter created by the tied-in structure below the knee limits strength of the flexor tendons so important to absorbing concussion and diffusing impact through the leg, making the horse more prone to tendon injury particularly at the midpoint of the cannon or just above the midpoint. Leverage of muscular pull is decreased as the tendons pull in against the back of the knee rather than in a straight line down the back of the leg. This reduces power and speed.
• This conformational characteristic is also often associated with a reduced size in the pisiform-shaped accessory carpal bone on the back of the knee over which the tendons pass. Small joints are at risk of injury while also not providing adequate support to the column of the leg under the stress of weight-bearing. (Refer also to Hocks Too Small for more detail.)

MANAGEMENT/TRAINING STRATEGIES:
Strengthening exercises of the hindquarters and back promotes the ability to shift the center of gravity somewhat to the rear and off the front limbs. Also, stretching exercises accomplished by encouraging the horse to stretch through the neck and back increase shoulder flexibility and improve gait efficiency.

BEST JOB FOR THIS HORSE:
Sports that shift the work effort more to the rear quarters or at least do not depend upon perfect forelimb conformation, such as dressage, reining, cutting, and driving.

Right: Notice how this horse's legs angle in just below the knee at the back of the leg. This is referred to as "tied-in." Anytime a horse's legs are not aligned correctly there is chance of damage to the smaller bones of the joints and legs.

Below: Endurance riding is not an ideal sport for a horse that is tied-in because of the stress it puts on the forelegs.

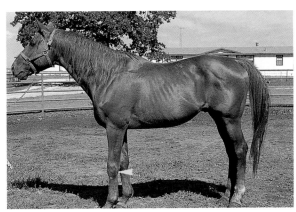

Photo by Nancy S. Loving, DVM

Above: A horse that is tied-in is better suited to sports that rely more on the hind end than the front such as reining and cutting.

Left: In dressage the ability to work in strong collection is critical. A horse with less than perfect forelegs will not be penalized.

Calf-Kneed/Back at the Knee

DESCRIPTION:
As seen in profile, the knee inclines backwards behind a straight plumb line dropped from the middle of the forearm to the fetlock.

HOW COMMON:
Uncommon.

BREEDS/ACTIVITIES MOST AFFECTED:
Racing, eventing, jumping, steeplechase, cutting, reining.

PERFORMANCE CONSEQUENCES:
• This knee conformation usually leads to unsoundness in horses participating in speed sports. Excess stress is placed on the front of the knee joints as the joint over-extends at fast speeds when the horse loads the leg with full weight. The backward angle of the knee causes compression fractures to the front surfaces of the bones in the knee joint, and ligamentous injury within the knee. The calf-kneed appearance worsens with muscle fatigue as the supporting muscles and ligaments above the knee lose their stabilizing function.
• The tilted back configuration of the calf-knee weakens the mechanical efficiency of the forearm muscles as they pull across the back of the carpus such that the so-afflicted horse has less power and speed than a normal, straight-legged individual. The tendons behind the knee and the check ligaments assume an excess load so are at risk of strain. Often the carpal bones are small and insufficient to diffuse concussion from impact.

MANAGEMENT/TRAINING STRATEGIES:
It is important that trimming and shoeing strategies focus on eliminating a long toe and low heel syndrome as this creates a functional calf-knee in a straight-kneed horse and worsens the situation for a true calf-kneed conformation. Muscle strengthening exercises for the forequarters are especially helpful to deter muscular fatigue. Such exercises include hill climbing and trotting cavallettis.

BEST JOB FOR THIS HORSE:
Sports that concentrate more on hindquarter function than impact on the front legs such as dressage, or slow-moving activities such as pleasure riding (trail or arena) that do not persist for long periods.

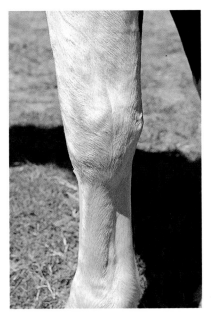

Left: This horse's knees are not in a straight line with the rest of his leg. Such conformation puts undo pressure on the knee itself, often resulting in soundness problems.

Below: A calf-kneed horse will have less power and speed than a straight legged horse.

Above: The backward angle of the calf-kneed horse can cause compression fractures to the front surfaces of the bones in the knee joint. High speed sports are not recommended for such a horse.

Above: Muscle strengthening exercises may be helpful for a calf-kneed horse, but he is not well suited for sports like cross-country galloping or jumping in which the front legs take a lot of pressure.

Bench or Offset Knees/Offset Cannons

DESCRIPTION:
The cannon bone is set to the outside of the knee so when viewed from the front, an imaginary plumb line dropped from the top of the leg to the ground does not fall through the middle of the knee.

HOW COMMON:
Common.

BREEDS/ACTIVITIES MOST AFFECTED:
All sports, but particularly speed activities.

PERFORMANCE CONSEQUENCES:
• The leg is most efficient at distributing stress when it works as a straight-line column. Offset cannon bones cause excessive stress on the lateral surfaces of the joints from the knee down and on the outside portions of the hoof.
• The medial splint bone normally assumes a weight-bearing function, but with bench knees, an exaggerated degree of the horse's weight is supported by the medial splint bone leading to the development of "splints." These are often associated with lameness, at least initially, and a cosmetic blemish remains.

MANAGEMENT/TRAINING STRATEGIES:
No specific strategies can correct or compensate for this conformational defect. This characteristic is often heritable so should not be continued through breeding stock.

BEST JOB FOR THIS HORSE:
Non-speed activities like pleasure riding, driving in harness, equitation showing.

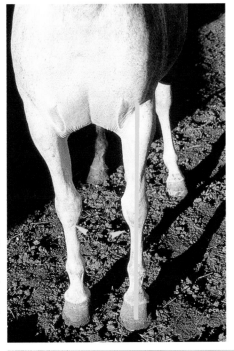

Photo by Nancy S. Loving, DVM

Bench knees occur when the cannon bone is set to the outside of the knee. If you were to draw a straight line from the top of the leg to the ground, it would not pass through the center of the knee.

A horse's leg works best when it is a straight column. Offset cannon bones put a great deal of stress on the inside of the knee joints and the inside hooves. Sports like cutting that require lateral moves are not ideal pursuits for the horse with bench knees.

Bucked, Sprung, or Goat Knees/Over in the Knees

DESCRIPTION:
As seen in profile, the knee inclines forward in front of a straight plumb line dropped from the middle of the forearm to the fetlock.

HOW COMMON:
Uncommon.

BREEDS/ACTIVITIES MOST AFFECTED:
Racehorses, steeplechasers, jumpers, eventers.

PERFORMANCE CONSEQUENCES:
• This conformation is often the result of an injury to the check ligament or to structures at the back of the knee. Because the knees buckle forward, the column of the leg is weakened. The horse is more apt to stumble and lose its balance due to reduced flexibility and extension of knee joints that always remain "sprung." If the condition is congenital, it is often related to poor muscular development on the front of the forearms which limits the speed and power of a horse's athletic abilities.

• Bucked knees are prematurely flexed so as they support weight more stress is applied to the tendons on the back of the leg, increasing the risk of developing a bowed tendon. The angle of attachment of the deep digital flexor muscle on the check ligament is increased, predisposing the check ligament to strain. Because the tendons (behind the cannon bone) and the fetlock are held in increased tension at all times, the horse is also predisposed to injury of the suspensory ligament (desmitis) and of the sesamoid bones on the back of the fetlock. The pasterns take on a more upright position which further stresses the fetlocks and the check ligaments.

MANAGEMENT/TRAINING STRATEGIES:
Strengthening of the shoulder and forearm muscles reduces muscular fatigue with exertion so no undue stress is placed on lower tendons and ligaments. This can be accomplished with cavalletti exercises that lift the legs, with hill climbs and down hill trail work, with lateral exercises such as leg-yield, half-pass, serpentines, and spiraling in and out on circles.

BEST JOB FOR THIS HORSE:
Non-speed activities, such as pleasure riding, trail riding, equitation.

This condition is often the result of an injury to a horse's check ligament or the back of the knee. The column of the leg is weakened when the knees buckle forward and a horse is more likely to fall. The injury is common in horses performing speed sports like racing.

Pasterns Long and Sloping

DESCRIPTION:
The pastern is long relative to the rest of the leg structure causing it to slope in a backwards direction. A pastern is considered too long if it exceeds more than three-quarters of the length of the cannon bone.

HOW COMMON: Common.

BREEDS/ACTIVITIES MOST AFFECTED: Speed events such as racing, polo, steeplechasing, hunting, jumping, eventing, and long distance-sports such as endurance riding, combined driving, and competitive trail.

PERFORMANCE CONSEQUENCES:
• Long, sloping pasterns have been favored by horsemen through the ages because they are able to diffuse the impact when a horse's feet hit the ground, thus giving a more comfortable, springy ride. However, an excessive length to the pastern takes this too far. The tendons and ligaments on the back of the cannon area are placed into extreme tension with each footstep, predisposing the horse to a bowed tendon or suspensory ligament injury. The suspensory ligament is strained because the fetlock joint is unable to straighten as the horse loads the limb with its weight.
• Excessively long pasterns are weak and unable to stabilize fetlock drop, so a horse is predisposed to ankle injury, particularly in speed events when the sesamoid bones experience extreme pressure from the pull of the suspensory ligaments across the back of the fetlock. This can result in sesamoid bone fractures and breakdown injuries.
• Long, sloping pasterns also may be associated with development of high or low ringbone over time. Increased drop of the fetlock causes more stress on the pastern and coffin joints, setting up conditions for development of arthritis.
• Because it requires more muscular effort for a horse to elevate a long, sloping pastern, such horses are not efficient at sprinting sports because of the time delay in getting their feet off the ground to accelerate.

MANAGEMENT/TRAINING STRATEGIES:
Horses with long, sloping pasterns should be shod with ample caudal foot support to provide a platform for each landing step that might minimize the drop of the fetlock. Toes should be squared back to ease breakover. Eggbar shoes may provide additional support to minimize strain on ligaments and tendons. Fitness is very important when undertaking athletic activities as fatigued muscles loose their stabilizing action on the lower structures of the limb so the tendons and fetlock are then more at risk of injury.

BEST JOB FOR THIS HORSE:
Pleasure riding, equitation, dressage.

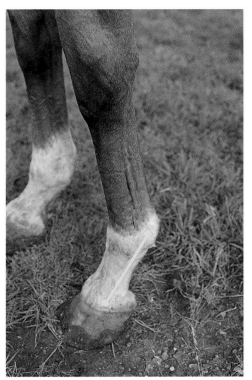

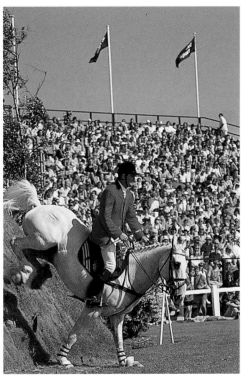

The long pastern bone connects the cannon bone to the short pastern bone and the bones of the hoof. If it is too long as seen here, it slopes backwards.

Jumpers with long sloping pasterns are at risk for lower leg injuries.

A long sloping pastern assures a comfortable ride. But a too long pastern, meaning one that is more than 3/4 the length of the cannon bone leaves a horse susceptible to bowed tendons or suspensory ligament injuries.

Pasterns Short and Upright

DESCRIPTION:
A pastern is considered too short if it is less than half the length of the cannon bone. The pastern is upright if it is angled more toward the vertical. On occasion, a pastern may be long and upright, having the same performance consequences as a short, upright pastern.

HOW COMMON:
Common.

BREEDS/ACTIVITIES MOST AFFECTED:
Quarter horses, Paint horses, Warmbloods.

PERFORMANCE CONSEQUENCES:
• A horse with a short, upright pastern is capable of rapid acceleration, but is restricted to a short length of stride. These horses are able to sprint rapidly from a standing start allowing them to excel in sprint sports. However, a short stride length is a product of both a short pastern and an accompanying upright shoulder to create short, choppy steps with minimal elasticity and limited speed for any distance.
• A short, upright pastern loses a great deal of shock-absorption capability leading to a more jarring ride and amplified stress on structures of the lower leg. Instead of the concussion being diffused across the entire foot as it would with a more sloping pastern, the concussion will be felt over the center of the foot directly over the navicular apparatus. A horse with this characteristic is more at risk of developing navicular disease, high or low ringbone, and sidebones due to excessive concussion impact and vibration within the bones and joints. Also, windpuffs or windgalls are common due to chronic irritation within the fetlock joint or flexor tendon sheath.
• A short, upright pastern has reduced mechanical efficiency for lifting and breaking over the toe, so the horse may tend to trip and stumble, particularly if the heels are sore and there is reluctance to lift the limb.

MANAGEMENT/TRAINING STRATEGIES:
Stretching exercises through neck and back to improve shoulder flexibility and strength through back and abdominal muscles to shift more weight rearward and off of the front end.

BEST JOB FOR THIS HORSE:
Sprint sports such as Quarter Horse racing, barrel racing, roping, reining, cutting.

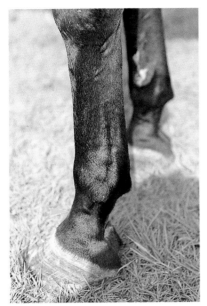

Left: An upright pastern is almost vertical rather than sloping backwards. If the pastern is less than half the length of the cannon bone it is considered short.

Below: A horse with short pasterns will have a short stride length.

The advantage of short pasterns is that they allow for fast acceleration as is needed for sprint racing, barrel racing, or roping.

Base Narrow: Toed-Out or Toed-In

DESCRIPTION:
As viewed from the front, a base narrow horse stands with the feet set closer in under the body than are the shoulders.

HOW COMMON:
Fairly common.

BREEDS/ACTIVITIES MOST AFFECTED:
Any breed. Any sport.

PERFORMANCE CONSEQUENCES:
• A base-narrow, toed-out horse stresses the outside structures of the limb, and particularly the outside of the foot. This combination of conformational problems causes the horse to move with a winging motion to the front feet, leading to interference injuries on the inside of the leg. This conformation also predisposes to plaiting or rope-walking (see text under Movement definitions.) The base-narrow, toed-out horse tends to hit itself more when muscles fatigue with hard work.
• A base-narrow, toed-in horse also places excessive strain on the lateral structures of the fetlock and pastern and on the outside of the hoof wall. This conformation causes a horse to paddle with the front legs. Although causing no interference problems, the motion appears busy and the horse's gait efficiency suffers.

MANAGEMENT/TRAINING STRATEGIES:
For the base-narrow, toed-out horse, interference boots will be necessary to prevent injuries to the medial splint bone, fetlock, and pastern. "Corrective" trimming usually worsens the condition by placing abnormal stress on other joints, so once the horse is past the age of surgical repair (2-9 months), it is best to level the feet at trimming. This horse should be trimmed as level as possible, with a bit of lowering of the inside wall necessary if it tends to grow too long relative to the wear of the outside wall. Be sure not to leave the shoes hanging beyond the inside hoof wall as the protruding branch further inflicts injury to the opposite leg. For the base-narrow, toed-in horse, the foot should also be leveled as much as possible.

BEST JOB FOR THIS HORSE:
Pleasure riding; not speed or agility events.

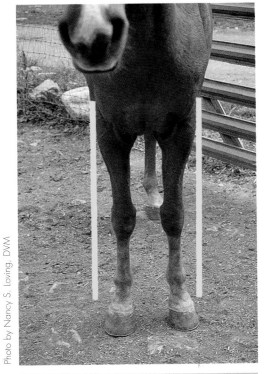

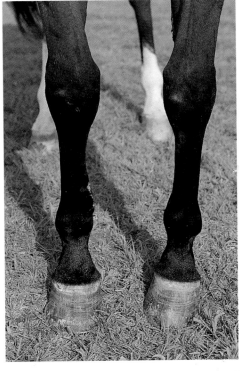

Above Left: When viewed straight on you can see that a base narrow horse's feet are set closer under the body than his shoulders. Such conformation puts excessive stress on the outside of the legs and feet.

Above Right: A horse that is base narrow, toed-in such as this one will paddle his front legs when in motion.

Left: The base narrow, toed-out horse actually wings his feet when he moves. This motion can cause injuries to the inside of his legs.

Base Wide: Toed-Out or Toed-In

DESCRIPTION:
Viewed from in front, the horse stands with feet placement wider than the shoulders. This is often associated with a narrow breast.

HOW COMMON:
Uncommon.

BREEDS/ACTIVITIES MOST AFFECTED:
Any sports.

PERFORMANCE CONSEQUENCES:
• A horse with a base-wide, toed-out conformation lands hard on the outside hoof wall while placing excessive strain on the medial structures of the fetlock and pastern leading to ringbone or sidebone, and potentially straining the medial structures of the carpus. This horse will wing with its front feet, leading to interference injury or overload injury of the medial splint bone.
• A horse with a base-wide, toed-in conformation lands hard on the inside hoof wall placing stress on the medial structures of the lower limb. This horse will paddle.

MANAGEMENT/TRAINING STRATEGIES:
The base-wide, toed-out horse needs slight lowering of the outside hoof wall as it tends to wear less than the inside wall. "Corrective" trimming usually worsens the condition by placing abnormal stress on other joints, so once the horse is past the age of surgical repair (2-9 months), it is best to level the feet at trimming.

BEST JOB FOR THIS HORSE:
Pleasure riding.

Far Left: The base-wide, toed-in conformation is fairly rare.

Left: When a horse is base-wide with toed-out conformation such as this, he puts strain on the medial structures of the fetlock and pastern when he moves. This can lead to ringbone or sidebone.

Above: This horse, with the toed-in conformation paddles his feet as he trots.

Above: The toed-out horse wings his feet at the trot and may injure the inside of his legs.

Toed-Out/Splay Footed

DESCRIPTION:
When viewed from the front a splay-footed horse's feet turn outward away from each other.

HOW COMMON:
Common.

BREEDS/ACTIVITIES MOST AFFECTED:
Any performance activity.

PERFORMANCE CONSEQUENCES:
• The toed-out conformation induces the hoof to move in a winging-in motion that predisposes the horse to interference injuries around the medial fetlock or medial splint bone. Such injuries create discomfort or lameness as well as leaving permanent cosmetic blemishes from scar tissue repair. Lameness may lead to a financial expense involved in lay-off time for the horse, while cosmetic or functional blemishes may reduce the value of the horse as a sale prospect.
• As the horse wings inward with a front foot, there is a chance the horse might step on itself, stumble, and fall. This poses a hazard to both horse and rider.
• A horse that is "tied-in behind the elbow" has restricted movement of the upper arm since there is less clearance of the arm bone (humerus) as it angles into the body too much. In such a case, reduced clearance of the legs with the body causes the horse to toe-out to compensate. This forced posture creates comparable problems as described above for the horse with true toed-out conformation.

MANAGEMENT/TRAINING STRATEGIES:
"Corrective" trimming usually worsens the condition by placing abnormal stress on other joints, so once the horse is past the age of surgical repair (2-9 months), it is best to level the feet at trimming. These horses tend to wear the inside hoof wall faster than the outside, so shoes may need to be applied to minimize excess wear to the foot that would lead to sole bruising. Interference boots minimize interference injury on the opposite leg.

BEST JOB FOR THIS HORSE:
Pleasure riding, low-impact work.

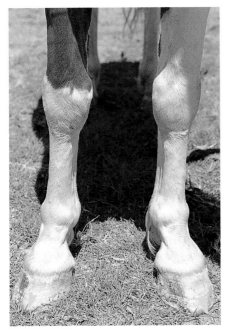

This horse is considered splay-footed because both front feet actually turn away from each other.

Splayed feet tend to move with a winging-in motion as can be seen here. This motion often causes injury to the medial fetlock or medial splint bone.

Toed-In/Pigeon-Toed

DESCRIPTION:
When viewed from in front, the horse stands with the toes of the hooves facing inward toward each other.

HOW COMMON:
Common.

BREEDS/ACTIVITIES MOST AFFECTED:
Any breed. Any sport.

PERFORMANCE CONSEQUENCES:
• A toed-in conformation causes excessive stress to be felt on the outside of the lower structures of the limb as the horse lands hard on the outside hoof wall. This often leads to degenerative arthritis of the pastern (high ringbone) or of the coffin joint (low ringbone). This horse is predisposed to sidebone and to sole bruising as well.
• The toed-in limb moves with a paddling motion, flinging the lower leg to the side before the horse sets it down. This is wasteful of energy and hastens fatigue so the horse has less stamina for prolonged physical activity.

MANAGEMENT/TRAINING STRATEGIES:
As with the toed-out horse, corrective trimming is ineffective after the horse has passed the opportune time for surgical repair (age 2-9 months). The best trimming strategy is to level the foot, and to shoe the foot to minimize excessive hoof wear and bruising on the lateral wall and sole.

BEST JOB FOR THIS HORSE:
Pleasure riding, low-impact work.

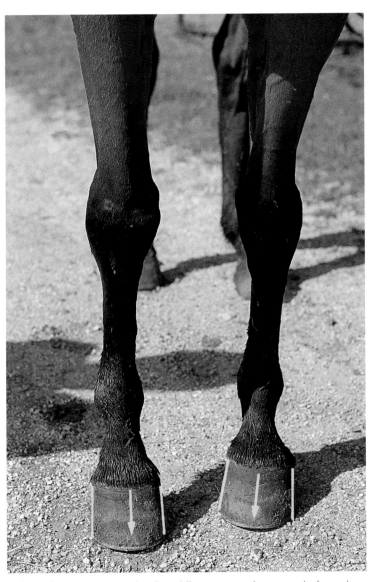

A horse that is pigeon-toed will paddle, meaning that instead of traveling in a straight line, his feet will arc out before landing in front of him.

Medial Carpal Deviation/Carpus Valgus/ Knock-Kneed

DESCRIPTION:
As viewed from the front, one or both knees (carpi) deviate inward toward each other, with the lower part of the leg angled out resulting in a toed-out stance. This angular limb deformity occurs because of unequal development of the growth plate of the distal radius, with the outside of the growth plate growing faster than the inside; the bottom of the forearm appears to incline inward.

HOW COMMON:
Common.

BREEDS/ACTIVITIES MOST AFFECTED:
Any horse is susceptible due to inheriting this as a conformational characteristic, but this may also be an acquired problem due to imbalanced nutrition leading to developmental orthopedic disease (DOD), or due to traumatic injury to the growth plate. Affects any sport.

PERFORMANCE CONSEQUENCES:
• As the knee deviates inward, the medial supporting ligaments of the carpus will be placed under excess tension. This may create soundness problems within the carpal joints or in the supporting ligaments of the joints.
• Due to a knock-kneed configuration, a horse with this conformation tends to toe-out from the carpus down. For performance problems related to toed-out conformation, refer to the section on Toed-out/Splay Footed.

MANAGEMENT/TRAINING STRATEGIES:
"Corrective" trimming usually worsens the condition by placing abnormal stress on other joints, so once the horse is past the age of surgical repair (about 6-9 months), it is best to level the feet at trimming. These horses tend to wear the inside hoof wall faster than the outside, so shoes may need to be applied to minimize excess wear to the foot that would lead to sole bruising. Interference boots minimize interference injury on the opposite leg.

BEST JOB FOR THIS HORSE:
Pleasure riding, low-impact work, low-speed events.

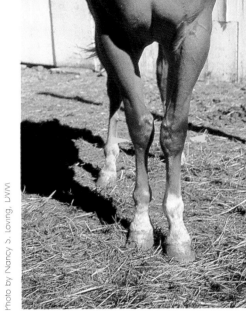
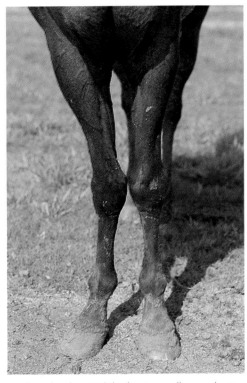

The knees (carpi) of both of these horses lean in toward each other. While this is usually an inherited problem, it can also result from imbalanced nutrition during growth.

Rotated Cannon Bone

DESCRIPTION:
When viewed from in front, the cannon bone rotates to the outside of the knee so that it appears slightly "twisted" in its axis relative to the knee joint. The leg may still be correct and straight in alignment of the joints with each other, but more often the cannon rotation is associated with an appearance of carpus valgus although the abnormality is not a result of growth-plate differences in the distal radius.

HOW COMMON:
Common.

BREEDS/ACTIVITIES MOST AFFECTED:
Any horse, any sport.

PERFORMANCE CONSEQUENCE:
Ideally, the long bones and joints follow a straight line beneath the horse to provide a straight column for weight-bearing support. The straightness of this column allows equal loading of the joints and ligaments side-to-side to diffuse stress down the limb. A rotated cannon places excess strain on the inside of the knee and lower joints of the leg, potentially leading to soundness issues.

MANAGEMENT/TRAINING STRATEGIES:
Trim and shoe the feet as level as possible, and provide adequate caudal heel support for the feet. Condition the horse well for the intended task.

BEST JOB FOR THIS HORSE:
Horses with rotated cannons uncommonly develop soundness problems directly related to this characteristic, so any work effort can be explored provided the horse is well conditioned and fit for the job so the muscles and joints can sustain the impact of exercise.

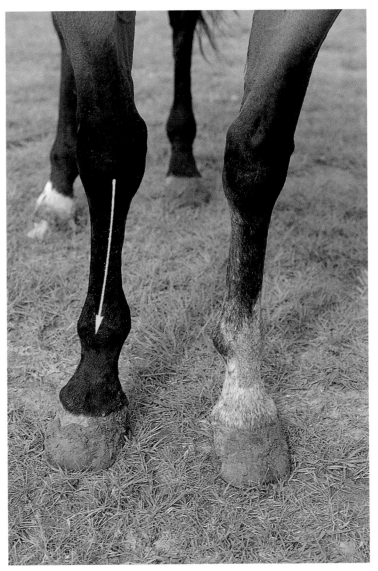

Rotation of the cannon bone gives the cannon a twisted appearance in relation to the knee joint. This condition places excess strain on the inside of the knee and lower leg joints, and may lead to soundness problems.

Toed-Out/Lateral Deviation of Pastern from Fetlock/ Fetlock Valgus

DESCRIPTION:
This is an angular limb deformity that creates a toed-out or duck-footed appearance from the fetlock down, with the toe pointing outward away from the opposite limb.

HOW COMMON:
Fairly common.

BREEDS/ACTIVITIES MOST AFFECTED:
Any athletic horse.

PERFORMANCE CONSEQUENCES:
• This type of angular limb deformity places excess stress on one side of the hoof, pastern, and fetlock joints with each landing step, predisposing the horse to degenerative joint disease (DJD or arthritis) such as ringbone and to foot soreness and bruising. A horse with this characteristic will tend to "wing" the foot when in motion. This inward arc of the hoof potentially hits the inside of the opposite front leg to create an interference injury. Persistent interference injury may damage the splint bone or the cannon bone, creating either cosmetic blemishes or functional problems such as a fracture of the splint bone.
• To develop speed at the trot and canter, a horse needs to land squarely on each foot, with each foot strike landing parallel to the body. Lateral deviation of a front foot diminishes the push from the rear legs as the symmetry and timing of the striding is altered with rotated foot placement, particularly at the trot. Stride efficiency is affected to slow the horse's gait. A horse with toed-out conformation is often unable to sustain years of hard work associated with a lot of impact stress. This limits athletic use to pleasure activities.

MANAGEMENT/TRAINING STRATEGIES:
This angular limb deformity is correctable with surgery if addressed before a foal is two months old; after this time, the growth plate has closed and the limb cannot be straightened. Then, it becomes a matter of trimming and shoeing to minimize the winging action of the foot. Often the outside wall and toe need to be rasped slightly lower to level the foot as the inside portions of the foot wear more quickly when the horse is barefoot. Protective leg boots should be worn to minimize interference injuries. Such a trait is generally heritable, and a horse with this type of conformation should not be used as breeding stock.

BEST JOB FOR THIS HORSE:
Pleasure work not involving speed or sustained impact.

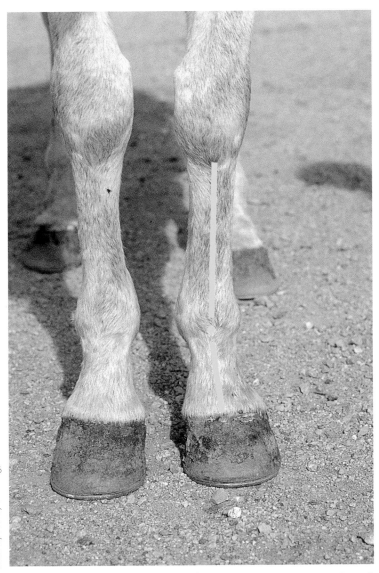

From the fetlock down, this horse's feet are toed-out. When moving he will "wing" his feet and put more stress on the side of his front hooves, pastern and fetlock joints. Such a horse is prone to degenerative joint disease.

Toed-In/Medial Deviation of Pastern/Fetlock Varus

DESCRIPTION:
This is an angular limb deformity that creates a pigeon-toed appearance from the fetlock down, with the toe pointing inward toward the opposite limb.

HOW COMMON:
Fairly common.

BREEDS/ACTIVITIES MOST AFFECTED:
Any breed. Affects any sport.

PERFORMANCE CONSEQUENCES:
• A horse with this characteristic will tend to "paddle" the foot when in motion. The outward arc of the hoof as it paddles creates excessive motion of the limb so as to exert twisting on the joints when the hoof is in the air. While visually unappealing for a show horse, this is wasteful of energy and reduces efficiency of the stride, with such a horse fatiguing more quickly than a straight-legged individual.
• As the hoof initially impacts the ground on the inside wall, considerable stress is assumed by the inside structures of the hoof and lower joints, potentially leading to ringbone (degenerative joint disease) and to sole and heel bruising of the inside hoof.

MANAGEMENT/TRAINING STRATEGIES:
Trim this horse as level as possible since "corrective" shoeing strategies are inappropriate after the horse has passed the age of two months when surgical correction is no longer an option. Shoe this horse with adequate caudal heel support to provide a good platform for foot placement. Rocker or roll the toes to ease breakover. Such a trait is generally heritable and a horse with this type of conformation should not be used as breeding stock.

BEST JOB FOR THIS HORSE:
Pleasure riding, non-impact work, low-speed sports, non-pivoting sports.

This hereditary deformity causes the horse's front feet to toe-in, making him pigeon-toed. Such a horse will paddle its feet when moving, and the inner sides of the hooves and lower joints will take extra stress. Such feet should be kept well trimmed.

Section 4
Feet

Feet Too Small

DESCRIPTION:
Relative to the size of the bone of the horse and to its body mass, the feet are proportionately small.

HOW COMMON:
Common.

BREEDS/ACTIVITIES MOST AFFECTED:
The propensity to breed for small feet is common in many breeds, but is especially noted in Quarter Horse types, Thoroughbreds (where it may be caused by trimming to make the hoof fit the shoe), and Saddlebreds. A small foot has direct performance consequences on any breed or in any sport.

PERFORMANCE CONSEQUENCES:
• The foot is a primary structure in shock-absorption for any horse in any sport. A small foot is far less capable of diffusing impact stress associated with each foot fall than is a large, elastic hoof.
• The small foot not only leads to increased impact felt throughout the limb, but on hard footing, the hoof itself receives extra punishment and concussion. Over time, this may lead to chronic sole bruising, concussion laminitis, heel soreness, navicular syndrome, and ringbone (degenerative joint disease). Sore-footed horses take short, choppy steps leading to a rough ride that lacks fluid and elastic gait efficiency.

MANAGEMENT/TRAINING STRATEGIES:
Horses with small feet need excellent and regular shoeing care. They often benefit from the support afforded by applying egg bar shoes. Synthetic (polyurethane) shoes have afforded many foot-sore horses a great degree of comfort by diminishing concussion absorbed in the foot. Such an undesirable characteristic is heritable; small-footed horses should be culled from breeding stock.

BEST JOB FOR THIS HORSE:
If given good shoeing support, a small-footed horse can tackle any sport, but soundness may suffer over time if persistent stress is incurred by the feet in sports like jumping, eventing, or distance trail riding. Sport events in soft footing (arena settings) such as equitation, cutting, reining, barrel racing, or dressage generally promote athletic longevity as compared with riding activities over hard-ground or downhill inclines.

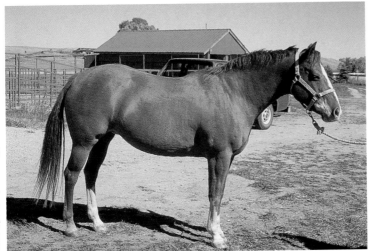

Photo by Nancy S. Loving, DVM

Left: Compared to his bone structure and bulky build, this horse's feet are quite small. Breeding for small feet is found in Saddlebreds, Thoroughbreds and Quarter horses.

Photo by Nancy S. Loving, DVM

With regular care and proper shoes a small-footed horse can do any sport but over time if he is constantly at work on hard surfaces or over rough terrain, he may develop soundness problems.

The horse's foot acts as a shock absorber and so a smaller foot naturally provides less cushion on impact than a larger one. Sports performed in an arena or in soft footing may be preferable for the small-footed horse.

Feet Large and Flat/ Puddle- or Mushroom-Footed

DESCRIPTION:
The feet are large in width and breadth in proportion to the body size and mass of the horse. Some horses may have slight pastern bones relative to large coffin bones, thus amplifying the visual size of the foot.

HOW COMMON:
Common.

BREEDS/ACTIVITIES MOST AFFECTED:
Any breed may be affected. A flat foot that is prone to bruising limits soundness in horses involved in concussion sports such as jumping, eventing, steeplechase, or distance riding.

PERFORMANCE CONSEQUENCES:
• A large foot is an attribute in a performance horse, but in some cases without proper shoeing support on certain ground, like sandy soils, the sole may flatten; low, flat soles are predisposed to bruising and/or laminitis. The horse would take short, choppy strides giving the appearance of "walking on eggs" or "walking on ice." Flat soles make it difficult for a horse to comfortably work on rocky or rugged footing without extra hoof protection.
• A large foot that has a good cup to the sole is the ideal foot for any horse as it absorbs concussion well and provides a good base of support for the limbs. Big-footed horses have less incidence of lameness problems associated with the front feet, and hold up well to athletic intensity over the years. Often a big-footed horse is also endowed with ample bone structure. (Refer to Insufficient Bone for more detail.)

MANAGEMENT/TRAINING STRATEGIES:
A flat-footed horse may need to always be shod in pads to protect the sole from bruising. Synthetic (polyurethane) shoes have afforded many foot-sore horses a great degree of comfort by diminishing concussion absorbed in the foot. Easy Boots placed over the shod foot also protect the soles of flat-footed horses for trail riding use.

BEST JOB FOR THIS HORSE:
Sports involving soft footing or short distances, like barrel racing, gymkhana, flat racing, equitation, or dressage.

While a large foot is beneficial for a performance horse, a flat foot is not. Flat-footed horses participating in impact sports like eventing and show jumping are prone to soundness problems.

Photo by Nancy S. Loving, DVM

While a big-footed horse can perform well in any sport, proper shoeing is critical, especially for the horse that performs in impact sports like endurance riding.

A large foot with a good cup to the sole is ideal. It provides an excellent base of support for the legs and such horses are at less risk of developing lameness problems related to the feet.

Mule Feet

DESCRIPTION:
A narrow, oval foot with steep walls is often found on mules and so described when found on the front feet of a saddle-horse.

HOW COMMON:
Fairly common.

BREEDS/ACTIVITIES MOST AFFECTED:
Quarter Horses, Arabians, Saddlebreds, Tennessee Walking horses, Foxtrotters, Mules.

PERFORMANCE CONSEQUENCES:
• A narrow, mule-shaped foot with its steep walls provides little shock absorption to the foot and the limb. This potentially creates soundness issues such as sole bruising, corns, concussion laminitis, navicular syndrome, sidebones, or ringbone. Not all mule-shaped feet have soundness problems particularly if the horse is light on the front end; in fact, some of these feet may be very tough and resistant in rocky terrain, providing the horse with nimbleness and agility on uneven footing.
• Note that the function of the hind feet is to assist forward propulsion of the horse so it is normal to see a narrower, mule-shaped hoof on the rear limbs as compared to the front. A deep cup to the sole improves the shock-absorption properties despite the foot being narrow.

MANAGEMENT/TRAINING STRATEGIES:
Good, supportive shoeing assists a mule-footed horse in sustaining impact over the miles.

BEST JOB FOR THIS HORSE:
Soft-terrain type sports, like polo, dressage, and other arena work (equitation, reining, cutting, roping), pleasure riding.

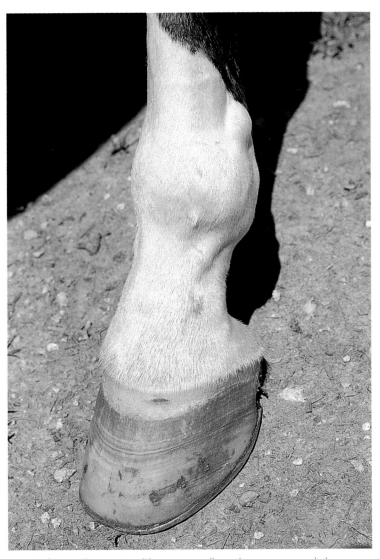

A mule foot is characterized by steep walls and a narrow, oval shape.
While this shape can cause soundness problems in some cases such a
foot is advantageous. For a light horse working over rough terrain as in
trail riding, a mule foot may be a sure foot.

Coon-Footed

DESCRIPTION:
Slope of the hoof wall is steeper than the slope of the pastern in a coon-footed horse. Often this is associated with excessively long, sloping pasterns tending to the horizontal, which breaks the angulation between the pastern and the hoof. Most commonly seen in the rear feet, especially in post-legged horses. This conformational trait has been noted by the author in the front feet of Paso Fino horses due to weak suspensory ligaments that allow fetlock drop.

HOW COMMON:
Uncommon.

BREEDS/ACTIVITIES MOST AFFECTED:
Any sports, particularly speed sports like racing, polo, steeplechasing, and eventing, and agility sports like cutting, reining, jumping.

PERFORMANCE CONSEQUENCES:
• A coon-footed horse suffers similar problems as the horse with a too long and too sloping pastern. The horse is prone to run-down injuries on the back of the fetlock. If foot lift off is delayed in sticky footing like mud or sand, ligament and tendon strain is likely as is an injury to the sesamoid bones of the fetlock.
• An inherent weakness to the supporting ligaments of the lower leg due to post-legged conformation or acquired injury to the suspensory ligaments will result in a coon-foot configuration as the fetlock drops, causing the pastern to slope obliquely in a more horizontal alignment than the front of the hoof wall.

MANAGEMENT/TRAINING STRATEGIES:
The foot should be shod with ample caudal foot support, and all efforts should be made to prevent the development of a long-toe, low-heel foot configuration which further stresses the joints, ligaments, and tendons of the lower leg. Support for the foot and the lower joints may be achieved by using eggbar shoes. Degree pads may be helpful for horses with suspensory ligament breakdown, but should be applied only after consultation with a veterinarian.

BEST JOB FOR THIS HORSE:
Low-speed exercise such as pleasure riding or equitation.

A horse is described as coon-footed if the slope of the hoof wall is steeper than the slope of the pastern, as seen here. The condition usually affects the hind feet but is relatively uncommon.

Problems of the coon-footed horse are similar to those found in a horse with long or sloping pasterns. Much of the impact is taken by the fetlock, as seen in the extreme drop of even this normal horse's fetlock as it trots.

Club Foot

DESCRIPTION:
The slope of the front face of the hoof exceeds 60 degrees. Often a club-footed hoof has long, upright heels. This syndrome may be a result of contracture of the deep digital flexor tendon that was not addressed at birth or that developed as a result of nutritional imbalances or trauma.

HOW COMMON:
Fairly common.

BREEDS/ACTIVITIES MOST AFFECTED:
Any athletic horse.

PERFORMANCE CONSEQUENCES:
• A club foot comes in various degrees of abnormal angulation, from slight to very pronounced. A horse with an obvious club foot tends to land more on the toes creating a risk of toe bruising or laminitis. Such a horse does poorly at prolonged exercise particularly over hard-packed or uneven terrain such as a trail horse or event horse would encounter.
• Because the toe is easily bruised, a club-footed horse often moves with a short, choppy stride, or may stumble. Such a horse would make a poor jumping prospect due to trauma incurred by the impact of landing even in a normal footed horse.

MANAGEMENT/TRAINING STRATEGIES:
Radiographs should be taken of the affected hoof to determine the alignment of the coffin bone within the hoof capsule so corrective measures can be taken to minimize trauma to the internal structures of the foot. Hereditary tendencies to this conformation should dictate these horses be culled from breeding stock.

BEST JOB FOR THIS HORSE:
Activities performed in soft footing or arena work such as dressage, equitation, pleasure riding; sports that depend upon strong hindquarter usage such as cutting, roping, or reining.

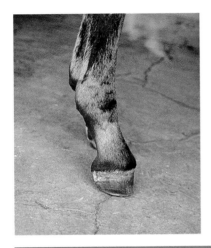

When the slope of a horse's hoof face is greater than 60 degrees he is described as club-footed. When moving, such a horse tends to land on his toes and may suffer bruising in the area or develop laminitis.

Photos by Nancy S. Loving, DVM

A club-footed horse often moves with short, choppy steps if his feet are sore or bruised. This may cause him to trip or stumble and riding over rough terrain is not recommended for such a horse.

A club-foot does not affect sports where hind impulsion is most important, like cutting or reining.

Contracted Heels

DESCRIPTION:
As viewed from behind or from the bottom of the foot, the heels appear narrow and the sulci of the frogs are deep while the frog may be atrophied.

HOW COMMON:
Common.

BREEDS/ACTIVITIES MOST AFFECTED:
Any breed can be affected, but especially Quarter Horses, Thoroughbreds, Saddlebreds, Tennessee Walking horses, or Gaited horses that have small feet relative to their body size.

PERFORMANCE CONSEQUENCES:
• Contracted heels are not normally an inherited conformation characteristic, but rather a symptom of a simmering limb unsoundness. A horse in discomfort or pain will "protect" the limb by landing more softly on it. Over time, the structures of the heel of the foot "contract" or narrow relative to the other foot, or relative to the inherit conformation of the horse. A source of pain should be explored by veterinary exam.
• Contracted heels may in themselves create health issues in the foot such as thrush since the narrowness of space between the heels traps debris. A contracted heeled hoof also is less expansible and elastic so it loses its shock-absorption capacity, leading to or exacerbating navicular disease, sole bruising, laminitis, or corns. In addition, a contracted foot may greatly restrict expansibility of the heels, leading to lameness due to pressure around the coffin bone and reduced elasticity of the digital cushion.

MANAGEMENT/TRAINING STRATEGIES:
A thorough veterinary exam should be pursued to identify the source of a horse's discomfort so appropriate corrective measures can be taken with shoeing or treatment of underlying joint or navicular pain. Shoes should be fit wide and should provide ample caudal foot support, such as found with eggbar shoes. Daily cleaning of the feet minimizes the chance for development of thrush related to poor hoof hygiene.

BEST JOB FOR THIS HORSE:
Non-concussion sports.

Left: Contracted heels are a symptom of an injury rather than a hereditary condition. The heels are narrow and the frog may become atrophied.

Below: In general horses with small feet are more likely to suffer from contracted heels and Quarter horses, Thoroughbreds, Tennessee Walkers and Gaited horses are most prone to the condition.

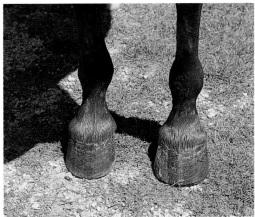

Photo by Nancy S. Loving, DVM

Above: When a horse has a sore foot he will "protect" it by landing more softly on it. If the injury isn't treated the heel of the foot will begin to contract.

Right: When a horse's foot contracts, it becomes less elastic and works less well as a shock absorber. This can cause real trouble for the horse who competes in sports like cross-country.

Thin Walls

DESCRIPTION:
The hoof wall is narrow and thin as viewed from the bottom. This is often associated with flat feet or feet too small for the horse's body size.

HOW COMMON:
Common.

BREEDS/ACTIVITIES MOST AFFECTED:
Quarter Horses, Thoroughbreds, Saddlebreds. Adversely affects any performance endeavor.

PERFORMANCE CONSEQUENCES:
• A thin, narrow wall reduces the weight-bearing base of support for the hoof and is often accompanied by flat or tender soles that easily bruise. Additionally, the hooves are subject to developing corns at the angles of the bar. Thin walled hooves tend to grow a long toe while growing very little heel, moving the hoof tubules in a more horizontal direction. This reduces the shock-absorption capacity of the hoof with increased risk of lameness.
• A narrow hoof wall has less integrity to accommodate expansion and flexion of the hoof, making it more brittle and prone to sand cracks and quarter cracks. The narrow white line also makes it hard for horseshoe nails to hold a purchase, so shoes are easily thrown and lost.

MANAGEMENT/TRAINING STRATEGIES:
Often a thin, narrow hoof wall can be encouraged to grow thicker by shoeing the horse with good hoof support, which minimizes the tendency to grow a long toe and low heel. This is achieved by rolling or rockering the toes to adequately square them back and by applying egg bar shoes or shoes with ample caudal support.

BEST JOB FOR THIS HORSE:
Work on soft footing, i.e. arena or grass activities.

The whitish area just inside the periphery of the hoof wall indicates that the hoof wall is thin and separated at the white line. This condition makes his hoof weaker and is often accompanied by flat soles that can bruise easily.

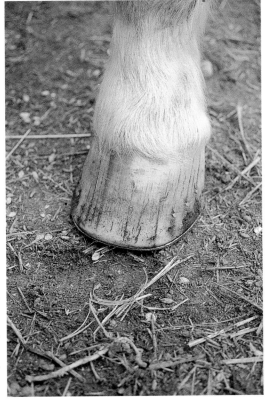

A narrow hoof wall is not very elastic and may crack easily. Correct shoeing can encourage the wall of the hoof to grow thicker.

Photo by Nancy S. Loving, DVM

Flared Hoof Wall

DESCRIPTION:
One side of the hoof wall flares toward the bottom of the hoof relative to a steep appearance on the other side of the same foot. The flared surface is concave; the steep surface may be convex.

HOW COMMON:
Common.

BREEDS/ACTIVITIES MOST AFFECTED:
Any breed. Any sport.

PERFORMANCE CONSEQUENCES:
• A flared hoof wall may be conformationally induced due to angular limb deformities or malalignments of the long bones with the hoof. These conformational problems create excess stress on one side of the hoof causing it to steepen, while the side with less impact grows a flare. The coronary bands often slope asymmetrically due to pushing up of the hoof wall and coronet on the steep side of the hoof which receives more impact than the flared side. The hoof may also develop sheared heels (one heel bulb pushed up relative to the other) which leads to lameness issues, contracted heels, and thrush.
• This foot configuration may be acquired by imbalanced trimming methods over time that stimulate more stress to be focused on one side of the hoof than the other.
• Chronic lameness may stimulate a horse to load the limb unevenly. Although the injury may be high in the limb, such as in a hock or stifle, the hoof wall will show signs of uneven impact over time.

MANAGEMENT/TRAINING STRATEGIES:
Excellent farrier care to balance the feet relative to the movement of the horse, not just visually balanced in a standing horse. Conformational concerns higher than the hoof need to be addressed to enable the horse to land as squarely as possible on the foot. (See discussion on each angular limb deformity problem.)

BEST JOB FOR THIS HORSE:
Low-impact or low-speed activities.

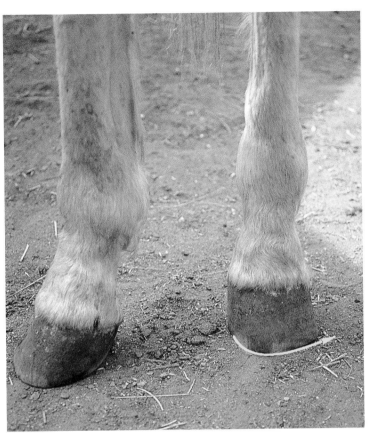

A flared hoof wall is the result of a skeletal deformity in the long bones of the hoof. As seen here, one side of the hoof flares out while the other side is steeper.

Hindquarters

Short Hindquarters

DESCRIPTION:
In the ideal horse, the length of the hindquarters as measured from the point of the hip to the point of the buttock is at least 30 percent of the length of the overall horse. A Thoroughbred may have hindquarter length nearing 35 percent. On average, hindquarter length ranges between 29 and 33 percent in most horses. Hindquarters are considered "short" if they are less than 30 percent of the horse's length.

HOW COMMON:
Common.

BREEDS/ACTIVITIES MOST AFFECTED:
Speed events like flat racing, steeplechasing, polo, and eventing or sports that require prolonged muscular effort and endurance like endurance riding, competitive trail, and combined driving.

PERFORMANCE CONSEQUENCES:
• The hindquarters of the horse is often referred to as the engine. The bigger the engine, the more "horsepower" available to propel and accelerate the horse across the ground. Insufficient length of the hindquarters minimizes the length of the muscles for powerful and rapid muscular contraction. Short quarters reduces speed over distance, sprint power, and stamina.
• A short hindquarter reduces the ability of a horse to fully engage the hindquarters to create collection important to dressage, or to brake in a sliding stop important to a cutting, reining, roping, or gymkhana horse.

MANAGEMENT/TRAINING STRATEGIES:
Exercises that encourage hindquarter development are important to improve strength, speed, and stamina of a weak quartered horse. Hill climbing helps develop these muscles, as do lateral exercises (leg-yield, half-pass) and active engagement of the back and hindquarters in collected work or sliding stops, and transitions between trot and canter.

BEST JOB FOR THIS HORSE:
Pleasure sports not requiring speed or power.

When a horse moves well his power comes predominantly from the hindquarters. Short hindquarters like this mean less power and speed. Hindquarters are measured from the point of the hip to the point of the buttocks and are considered short if they are less than 30% of the horse's length.

Top-level dressage work takes great strength and power. A horse with short hindquarters may be more challenged to perform well in collection.

Goose- or Steep-Rumped

DESCRIPTION:
When viewed from the side, the pelvis assumes a steep, downward slope.

HOW COMMON:
Uncommon.

BREEDS/ACTIVITIES MOST AFFECTED:
Common in draft horses. Sprint events.

PERFORMANCE CONSEQUENCES:
• The steep slant of the pelvis in effect lowers the point of the buttocks bringing it closer to the ground and shortening the length of muscles between the point of the buttock and the gaskin. A steep pelvis shortens the backward swing of the leg because of reduced extension and rotation of the hip joint. Ample range of motion in the hip joint is critical to speed at the gallop and to generating mechanical efficiency of the hip and croup muscles for power and thrust of the haunches. A goose-rumped horse is poor at sprinting and at flat racing because of diminished speed and power.
• The extreme slope of the pelvis, croup, and hip make it more difficult for a horse with this characteristic to get "under itself" to engage the haunches. This causes the loins and lower back to work harder, predisposing to injury of the lower back.
• A relatively steep pelvis is an advantage for sports that require rapid turns and spins, like reining or cutting. And, a steep pelvis is able to generate power for short, slow steps as seen in draft horse work.

MANAGEMENT/TRAINING STRATEGIES:
Activities that strengthen the haunches such as hill climbing, lateral work and collection, and trotting cavallettis are instrumental in developing hindquarter muscles. Development of the back and abdominal muscles relieves some of the work effort of the haunches. This can be accomplished with dressage exercises, cavallettis, jumping grid exercises.

BEST JOB FOR THIS HORSE:
Stock horse work, like reining or cutting; slow power events, like draft in harness; low-speed sports like equitation, pleasure riding, trail riding.

Left: Notice the steep, downward slope of this horse's hind end. A steep pelvis will limit the horse's ability to swing the hind legs backward because the muscles are shorter.

Below Left: This horse is not able to extend his legs behind him because of his goose-rumped conformation.

Above: The slope of the pelvis, croup and hip make it hard for a horse to engage his hind end. Consequently his loins and lower back will try to compensate and he'll be prone to injuries there.

Left: For draft horses a steep-rumped conformation is actually helpful because they can "dig in" with their haunches to help pull a heavy load.

Cat-Hammed/Frog's Thighs

DESCRIPTION:
Poor development of hindquarter muscles particularly along the quadriceps and thighs to create a feline appearing hind end configuration. Cat-hammed thighs often go hand-in-hand with other undesirable conformational characteristics including a goose-rump and sickle hocks. (Refer to these characteristics for more detail.)

HOW COMMON:
Uncommon.

BREEDS/ACTIVITIES MOST AFFECTED:
Seen most often in Gaited horses.

PERFORMANCE CONSEQUENCES:
• A cat-hammed horse lacks development of the hind-end muscles that are responsible for speed and power, so the horse lacks the inherent ability to be fast or strong. This reduces the usefulness of such a horse for sports like polo, eventing, jumping, steeplechase, and timber, flat, and harness racing.
• The gait of such horses tends to be more ambling than driving at the trot, and the horse often develops a stiff torso and back, making for a rigid, inelastic ride.

MANAGEMENT/TRAINING STRATEGIES:
In some cases, a cat-hammed horse is so conformed as a result of too many idle years in small confinement. These horses need diligent work at developing the rear musculature through conditioning on hills, trotting cavallettis and jumping grid gymnastic exercises, and with the use of lateral work to develop inner and outer muscles of the thighs.

BEST JOB FOR THIS HORSE:
Pleasure riding or driving.

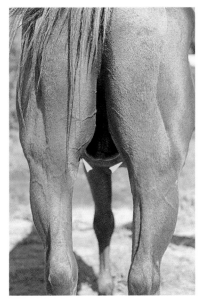

This horse's hind end appears weak and underdeveloped.

Horses can develop cat-hams if they are confined to small spaces. Conditioning with hill climbs, cavaletti work, and jumping grids will help build up the muscles.

Tipped Vulva

DESCRIPTION:
A tipped vulva describes the relationship of the anus and vulva in a mare, with the anus located forward of the vulva rather than directly over or slightly behind it.

HOW COMMON:
Common.

BREEDS/ACTIVITIES MOST AFFECTED:
Flat racing. Any breeding mare.

PERFORMANCE CONSEQUENCES:
• Because the anus is set forward of the vulva, feces can drop or leak into the vagina to create a chronic uterine infection that renders a mare infertile. In some cases, a tipped vulva occurs secondary to poor body condition and lack of nutrition that is accompanied by poor rear-quarter muscling, which causes the vulva to "tip forward."
• A tipped vulva is often associated with "windsucking" in racing Thoroughbred mares, a condition where air is sucked into the vagina when the horse is running at speed. The turbulence of air entering the vagina creates a "sucking" sound.

MANAGEMENT/TRAINING STRATEGIES:
Adequate nutrition and good body condition provide sufficient bulk and muscling to the haunches to prevent an artificially tipped vulva. A Caslick's surgery can be performed to stitch closed the top portion of the vulva so air and feces can't enter the vagina. All efforts should be made to cull mares with tipped vulvas from breeding stock as uterine infections generate unnecessary expense of medical treatment in efforts to get a mare pregnant.

BEST JOB FOR THIS HORSE:
Any performance job is appropriate as this is only of cosmetic significance or relates to breeding soundness. Perineal conformation is heritable so should be considered when using a mare as breeding stock.

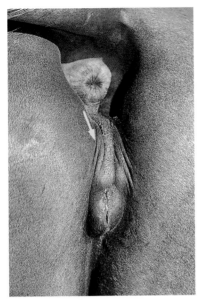

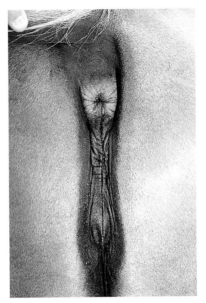

A normal vulva sits directly beneath a mare's anus. A tipped vulva angles in like this, letting feces leak into the vagina, causing infections.

This is the normal vulva position. Surgery can be performed to close the top part of a tipped vulva to avoid potential health problems.

On the track, Thoroughbred mares with tipped vulvas often experience a condition called "windsucking," in which air is sucked into the vagina when the horse is racing.

Narrow Hips

DESCRIPTION:
As viewed from the rear, the breadth between the hips is narrow.

HOW COMMON:
Common.

BREEDS/ACTIVITIES MOST AFFECTED:
Any breed can be affected, but Quarter Horse types tend not to have narrow hips. Mostly seen in Thoroughbreds, Saddlebreds, Gaited horses, and Arabians.

PERFORMANCE CONSEQUENCES:
• A narrow pelvis contributes to speed since a horse is able to get its hind legs well under its body to develop thrust. The shape of the hips is partly dictated by exercise development of haunch muscles or lack thereof.
• Sufficient width of the hindquarters provides ample breadth between the stifles, hocks, and lower legs to enable power, acceleration, and foot purchase into the ground, and thereby prevents interference injuries. Too narrow a pelvis limits the size of muscular attachments of the hips and adversely affects strength and power.

MANAGEMENT/TRAINING STRATEGIES:
Conditioning and strengthening of rear end muscles develops them to an appearance in proportion to the rest of the body.

BEST JOB FOR THIS HORSE:
Trail riding, carriage driving in harness, flat racing.

Narrow hips are fairly common in Thoroughbreds, Gaited horses and Arabians. When properly conditioned the rear end muscles can be developed in proportion to the rest of the horse's body.

A horse with a narrow pelvis can get his legs up under his body for a strong thrust. Such conformation is ideal for a race horse.

Rafter Hips

DESCRIPTION:
A rafter hip is a wide, flat hip that is shaped like a T when viewed from behind. Cattle tend to have this type of pelvis in the extreme.

HOW COMMON:
Uncommon.

BREEDS/ACTIVITIES MOST AFFECTED:
Gaited horses, Saddlebreds, and Arabians.

PERFORMANCE CONSEQUENCE:
The configuration of this hip type often is amplified by poor muscling along the thighs and lower hips.

MANAGEMENT/TRAINING STRATEGIES:
Any effort that improves muscling of the haunches, hips, and thighs such as hill climbs, trotting cavallettis, jumping grid gymnastics, correct riding with back elevated and haunches engaged.

BEST JOB FOR THIS HORSE:
Pleasure riding, light trail riding.

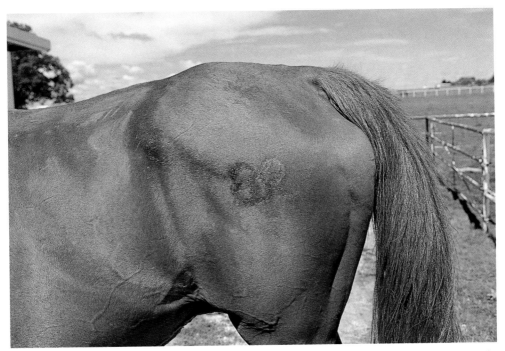

Rafter hips are angular and shaped like a T when viewed from behind. This horse's muscular condition can be improved with exercises for the hindquarters such as hill climbing, trotting cavalettis, and jumping gymnastics.

One Hip Bone Lower/Knocked-Down Hip

DESCRIPTION:
When viewed from behind, the point of the hip of one side is lower than the point of the hip on the other side. This may be due to injury to the point of the hip, or to subluxation or fracture of the pelvis.

HOW COMMON:
Uncommon.

BREEDS/ACTIVITIES MOST AFFECTED:
Any horse of any breed.

PERFORMANCE CONSEQUENCES:
• This characteristic is generally induced by a traumatic blow to the hip such as occurs when a horse runs into the side of a barn, or a post as the horse runs past the obstacle. This is brought to your attention because a knocked-down hip has performance consequences despite not being a heritable characteristic. The symmetry of the gait is affected, which has significant ramifications in a dressage horse or show horse. Interference with power and thrust created by normal synchronous muscular movement of the hip muscles may alter strength in jumping high fences, or may reduce speed important to a racehorse.
• A horse with a knocked-down pelvis is also more prone to developing muscular or ligamentous soreness associated with re-injury or strain to the damaged area. This is particularly likely to occur in a jumping horse, steeplechase horse, race horse, or event horse. However, in most cases in which the point of the hip has been crushed by a blow, the horse recovers completely and is able to continue performance work.

MANAGEMENT/TRAINING STRATEGIES:
Development of the haunch muscles is important through strengthening exercises like hill climbs, transitions between trot and canter and canter and trot, cavalletti exercises, jumping gymnastic grids.

BEST JOB FOR THIS HORSE:
Slow-speed sports, pleasure riding, trail riding.

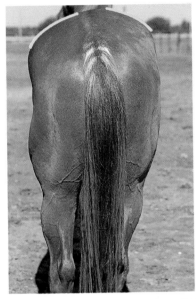

You can see that this horse's left hip sits lower than his right and that his hip and thigh muscles are atrophied. This condition is usually the result of an injury.

Photo by Nancy S. Loving, DVM

When a horse's hips do not sit evenly, his gaits are also uneven and he will not have the hind end power needed for sports like show jumping or dressage.

163

High Stifles/Short Hip

DESCRIPTION:
The ideal hip forms an equilateral triangle formed by imaginary lines drawn between the point of the hip, the point of the buttocks, and the stifle. A short hip represents a short femur (thigh bone), which reduces the length of the quadriceps and thigh muscles. The femur is short when the stifle appears "high," that is the stifle sits above the sheath on a male horse.

HOW COMMON:
Common.

BREEDS/ACTIVITIES MOST AFFECTED:
Any breed can be affected, but often seen in racing Quarter Horses or Thoroughbreds.

PERFORMANCE CONSEQUENCES:
• A short femur is effective in generating short, rapid, and powerful strokes important to sprint activities or draft work. Such hips are able to initiate "first gear" for rapid thrust and initiation of sprint speed.
• Ideally, the bones of the gaskin and femur should be of similar length in a horse that performs anything other than sprinting or draft sports. A short femur reduces stride length behind as well as elasticity of stride, which are important features to jumpers, flat or harness racers, and dressage horses.

MANAGEMENT/TRAINING STRATEGIES:
Exercises to equalize the weight distribution between front and rear ends improve the character of the gait and relieves some of the choppy, stabbing strokes of the rear legs.

BEST JOB FOR THIS HORSE:
Sprint sports or draft work.

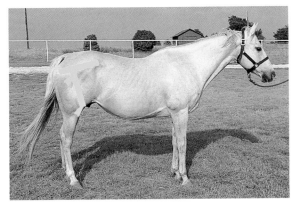

A horse with a short hip has a short femur or thighbone and this means the muscles in the thigh and quadriceps will also be shorter.

A short femur is advantageous for sports that require quick bursts of speed like roping or barrel racing.

Short hips act like a first gear in a horse allowing him to accelerate quickly. While it is seen in all breeds, this conformation is most common in Quarter horses.

Low Stifles/Long Hip

DESCRIPTION:
A long hip is created by a long femur which drops the level of the stifle to or below the sheath line on a male horse.

HOW COMMON:
Common.

BREEDS/ACTIVITIES MOST AFFECTED:
Favorable for all sports and breeds except sprinting or draft horses.

PERFORMANCE CONSEQUENCES:
• A long hip enables a horse to develop lots of speed and power after it gets moving, similar to the acceleration seen with a car once it reaches third or fourth gear. This is advantageous to flat racing, harness racing, eventing, steeplechasing, timber racing, eventing, endurance riding, and trail riding.
• The muscles of the hip, haunches, and thighs will be proportionately long with a long hip bone, giving them the capacity to develop speed and power by contracting over a sizable distance. This produces a ground-covering and efficient stride in all gaits.

MANAGEMENT/TRAINING STRATEGIES:
A long hip is a desirable conformational feature so normal conditioning and fitness programs should be pursued to maximize the athletic capabilities of the horse.

BEST JOB FOR THIS HORSE:
Eventing, jumping, steeplechase and timber racing, flat and harness racing, and distance trail events.

A long hip is created by a long femur bone. The longer bone places the stifle at or below the line of the sheath in a male horse.

While a short hip is good for quick bursts of speed, a long hip enables a horse to work with power and speed over the long haul. Such conformation is favorable in horses who flat race, event, steeplechase, or participate in endurance events. Here a long hip provides power for dressage exercise.

Short Gaskin/Hocks High

DESCRIPTION:
A short gaskin or high hocks indicates a relatively short tibia with a long cannon bone. In the ideal conformation, the hocks are placed slightly higher than the front knees with the point of the hock level with the chestnut of the front limb, but on a horse with this conformation, the hocks will be noticeably higher in placement. In its exaggerated form, the horse will have a downhill balance with the croup higher than the withers.

HOW COMMON:
Common.

BREEDS/ACTIVITIES MOST AFFECTED:
Thoroughbreds, racing Quarter Horses, Gaited horses.

PERFORMANCE CONSEQUENCES:
• A short gaskin and a long cannon allows a horse to pull its hind legs well beneath the body to give a long reach of rear stride. However, the hind legs do not always move in synchrony with the front legs. The result would be a relatively inefficient gait as the hind end is forced to slow to allow the front end to catch up, or the horse slows the hind end by taking high steps behind, giving a flashy, stiff hock and stifle action. Otherwise, the horse might forge or over-reach, inflicting injury to the back of the front feet or ankles.
• A short gaskin and long cannons often results in a sickle hock conformation with its ensuing problems. (Refer to Sickle-Hocked for more detail.)

MANAGEMENT/TRAINING STRATEGIES:
Exercises to improve a horse's rhythm at the trot and canter will facilitate synchronous movement of the front and hind end. Such exercises include arena work that encourages engagement of the back and hindquarters, serpentines, spiral in and out of a circle at trot, cavalletti trotting, and gymnastic jumping grids.

BEST JOB FOR THIS HORSE:
With proper training, such a horse can perform any pleasure or showing pursuit, trail riding, or driving with relative ease.

Ideally a horse's hocks should sit slightly higher than the point of the horse's knees, even with the chestnuts. High hocks are considerably higher and are accompanied by a long rear cannon bone.

This conformation allows the horse to have a very long stride in his hind legs, but they will not always synchronize with his front legs. Exercises that work on collecting can help correct this problem.

Long Gaskin/Low Hocks

DESCRIPTION:
A long gaskin is created by a long tibia (bone between the stifle and hock) while a low hock is associated with short cannon bones. The overall appearance is a rear end that tends to a squatting position.

HOW COMMON:
Common.

BREEDS/ACTIVITIES MOST AFFECTED:
Racing Thoroughbreds, stock horses.

PERFORMANCE CONSEQUENCES:
• A short cannon bone is desirable in any performance horse, but the long gaskin causes the hocks and lower leg to be placed behind the body in a camped out position. In order for the horse to get its hocks beneath the body to develop thrust, the lower leg must "sickle" or stand "cow-hocked." (See Sickle Hocks, Cow Hocks, and Camped Out Behind for more detail on consequences.)
• The long lever arm created by a long gaskin reduces the muscle efficiency to drive the rear limbs forward. The long gaskin makes it more difficult for a horse to engage the hindquarters and control rear limb movement important to exercise of a slow, regular rhythm like dressage. In addition, the rear legs may be unable to reach forward to step into the tracks of the front limbs, leading to a horse with a reduced rear limb stride length. A short stride behind forces the horse to take short steps in front despite having a good front limb conformation.

MANAGEMENT/TRAINING STRATEGIES:
Horses with long gaskins benefit from strengthening exercises for the muscles of the thigh and gaskin so these muscles can stabilize abnormal forces on the hocks. This is accomplished with lateral work such as half-pass, leg-yield, spiraling in and out of circles at trot and canter, and with hill climbs at trot and canter.

BEST JOB FOR THIS HORSE:
Galloping events like eventing, steeplechase, flat racing; sprinting sports that depend on rapid takeoff for a short distance, like racing Quarter Horses, cutting, reining, roping; draft events of short thrust in slow motion.

Left: When the bone between the stifle and the hock is long a horse is said to have a long gaskin. Racing and disciplines that require short bursts of speed are not a problem for a horse with long gaskins. Low hocks are found with short cannon bones.

Below Left: Strengthening exercises that include lateral work and work on hills at the trot and canter will help a horse with long gaskins by strengthening the muscles of the thigh and gaskin and protect the hocks from abnormal stress.

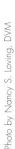

Photo by Nancy S. Loving, DVM

Above: A short cannon bone is preferable, but the long gaskin pushes the horse's hind legs out behind, making it difficult for him to engage his hind end for disciplines like dressage.

Left: A horse with long gaskins is often short-strided behind, causing him to take smaller steps in front even though the front legs may be in good conformation.

Hocks Too Small

DESCRIPTION:
The hock joints appear small relative to the breadth and size of the long bones above and below. The same principles described also apply to small knee joints in the front leg.

HOW COMMON:
Uncommon.

BREEDS/ACTIVITIES MOST AFFECTED:
Any horse, any sport, particularly speed or jumping events and sports requiring rapid turns, spins, or braking off the hind end, like cutting, reining, roping.

PERFORMANCE CONSEQUENCES:
• Strong, large joints are valuable to any performance horse since the joints form the fulcrum over which tendons and muscles pass to generate power and speed, and large joints absorb concussion and diffuse the load of the horse's mass. Small joints are more prone to developing degenerative joint disease (DJD) from concussion and instability, particularly in events in which the horse spends a considerable amount of time working off its hocks, like dressage, reining, cutting, and roping.
• A small hock often does not have a long tuber calcis (point of the hock) over which the tendons pass to create a fulcrum for development of power from the muscles. Small hocks limit the mechanical advantage required to propel a horse to run at speed. The breadth of the gaskin muscles is also dependent on the size and width of the hock. With a small hock, the gaskin muscles will be proportionately small and unable to generate speed and acceleration.

MANAGEMENT/TRAINING STRATEGIES:
Development of the haunches facilitates ease of muscular effort to reduce the work of the gaskin muscles and hocks and to minimize fatigue. This trait is heritable so conscientious efforts should be made to cull horses with small joints from breeding stock.

BEST JOB FOR THIS HORSE:
Slow working events, such as pleasure riding, light trail riding, equitation, dressage.

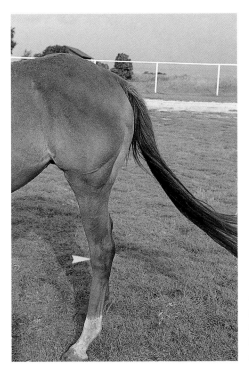

You always look for large joints in a performance horse because this is the path over which the tendons and muscles pass that give him his power and speed. The larger these are, the more powerful. And small joints like these hocks are more likely to develop degenerative joint disease.

Sports like cutting and reining are most affected by small hocks because so much of the quick turns and stops required come from a horse's ability to work off his hind end and hocks.

Cut Out Under the Hock

DESCRIPTION:
As viewed from the side, the front of the cannon bone where it joins the lower part of the hock appears small and weak compared to the size of the hock. In the front end, a similar phenomenon is seen as "tied in behind the knee."

HOW COMMON:
Uncommon.

BREEDS/ACTIVITIES MOST AFFECTED:
Can affect any breed. Will affect any sporting horses participating in activities that depend on strong hocks, like stock work, dressage, jumping.

PERFORMANCE CONSEQUENCES:
• The "cut out" beneath the front face of the hock actually reduces the diameter of the hock and cannon bones. This weakens the strength and stability of the hock joints in a similar manner as the consequences seen with small hocks described above. The cut-out structure means the hocks are less able to support the twisting motion seen with pirouettes of dressage, the roll-backs of reining and cutting, the sudden stops of roping, and the sudden turns of polo. Any horse with this characteristic that participates in dressage, roping, reining, cutting, polo, or jumping pursuits is at greater risk of incurring injury or arthritis of the hocks.

MANAGEMENT/TRAINING STRATEGIES:
Conditioning is essential to build strong haunch and back muscles to minimize muscular effort in the intended sport. Ease of effort puts less strain on all musculoskeletal structures, in this case hopefully sparing the stress applied to the hock joints. The horse should always be warmed up well and cooled down sufficiently to minimize muscular and tendon injury.

BEST JOB FOR THIS HORSE:
Pleasure work and equitation; any sport provided the horse is fit and up to the task.

Left: A horse is said to be cut out under the hock when the front of the cannon bone looks small and dips in slightly toward the back.

Below Left: While any breed can be affected by this conformation problem, the effects will be most noticeable in sports requiring strong hocks such as dressage, jumping, cutting and reining.

Above: Sports like reining that require quick changes of direction and twisting are not recommended for a horse cut out under the hock as he will be prone to injury and can develop arthritis of the hocks.

Left: The cut out structure of the hocks means that the hocks are weaker because the diameter of the hock and cannon bones is smaller. A horse cut out under the hock and performing a pirouette like this will be predisposed to developing degenerative joint disease.

Camped Out Behind

DESCRIPTION:
In the ideal horse as viewed from the side, a plumb line dropped from the point of the buttock should fall directly in line with the back of the rear cannon and fetlock. In this conformation, the cannon and fetlock stand "behind" the plumb line when the horse is squared up. This conformation is often associated with upright rear pasterns.

HOW COMMON:
Common.

BREEDS/ACTIVITIES MOST AFFECTED:
Any breed, but particularly seen in Gaited horses, Morgans, and Thoroughbreds.

PERFORMANCE CONSEQUENCES:
• If the alignment from the point of the buttock down is not "straight" along the plumb line, the horse's rear leg will move with a greater swing than normal before the foot contacts the ground. Not only does this create wasteful motion that hastens muscular fatigue and reduces stride efficiency, but there will be increased oscillation and vibrations felt through the joints, tendons, ligaments, and hooves. As a result the horse may develop quarter cracks in the rear feet and, with time, degenerative arthritis in any of the rear limb joints.
• A camped out behind horse has difficulty in bringing its hocks and cannons beneath the body unless it creates a functional sickle-hocked or cow-hocked configuration. The trot is inhibited by the long, overangulated legs with the horse tending to trot with a flat stride with the legs strung out reminiscent of the kick of a cross country skier. It is difficult for such a horse to engage the back or haunches, making upper level dressage movements or jumping bascule difficult to achieve, and making it difficult to efficiently gallop with speed. The back is susceptible to injury.

MANAGEMENT/TRAINING STRATEGIES:
Any exercises directed toward development of back and abdominal muscles will help this horse more effectively coil the loins to use the rear quarters to propel its body across the ground in a more efficient manner.

BEST JOB FOR THIS HORSE:
Pleasure work, trail riding, driving in harness.

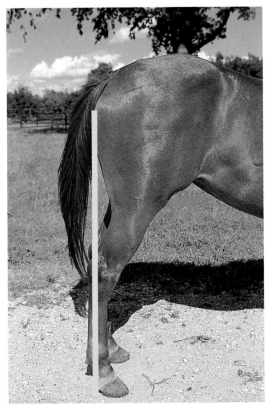

Left: This horse is squared up yet his hind legs are out behind him. This is referred to as being camped out behind.

Below: Upper level dressage with its required collection may prove difficult for a horse camped out behind. He will not be able to get his hind end underneath him without becoming sickle-hocked or cow-hocked.

Above: When a horse is camped out behind, its hind legs swing out behind before hitting the ground. This condition may cause arthritis over time from increased muscle fatigue and extra pressure on the joints.

Sickle- or Sabre-Hocked/Overangulated Long Hind Legs

DESCRIPTION:
This describes a "crooked" hind leg that slants slightly forward of a straight plumb line when viewed from the side, with the cannon unable to be placed in a vertical position giving the leg a "sickled" appearance. This conformation is often referred to as a "curby" hock as the potential exists for straining the plantar ligament on the rear, lower part of the hock to develop a "curb."

HOW COMMON:
Common.

BREEDS/ACTIVITIES MOST AFFECTED:
Hunters, eventers, racehorses, harness racers, polo ponies, and jumping horses.

PERFORMANCE CONSEQUENCES:
• In order to develop strong thrusting power and speed, the hock must be able to straighten as the horse propels the hindquarters forward. Sickle hocks limit straightening and backward extension of the hocks, thereby limiting push-off, propulsion, and speed so important to the activities mentioned above. The landing phase coming off a jump creates a dynamic sickle-hocked conformation even in a straight-legged horse, so it is best not to start with legs that are already sickled as this places additional stress on the hock and stifle joints.
• Folk tales once claimed this characteristic would better enable a horse to "sit down" on its haunches for agile maneuvering such as needed in roping, reining, and cutting horse activities, or for draught work. However, due to the closed angulation and loading stresses placed on the back of the hock by this conformational characteristic, a horse with this structure is predisposed to degenerative joint disease (bone spavin), distention of the tibiotarsal joint (bog spavin), thoroughpin (distention of the Achilles tendon sheath just above the hock), and curb (strain of the plantar ligament). For most pleasure horse activities, sickle hocks do not interfere with performance directly unless the horse develops DJD or tendon or ligament strain as a consequence.

MANAGEMENT/TRAINING STRATEGIES:
The horse should be shod with ample rear foot support to provide a solid platform for limb placement and to give a better foot purchase for push-off. Toes should be squared off to ease breakover and to reduce delay of foot lift from the ground. Training should address development of a strong topline and abdominal muscle as well as quadriceps and thigh strength. In this way, exercise requiring hind limb engagement is achieved with as little muscular effort as possible.

BEST JOB FOR THIS HORSE:
Non-speed sports.

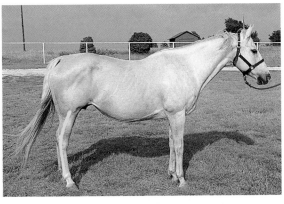

Right: The lower hind legs of this horse slant forward slightly in what is called a sickle-hocked conformation.

Below: For most pleasure riding, sickle hocks would not hinder a horse's performance.

Above: The loading stresses placed on the back of the hocks in the tight maneuvers needed for roping and reining make horses with sickle hocks more prone to degenerative joint disease as well as strained tendons and ligaments.

Above: Sickle hocks limit the straightening and backward extension of the hocks that the horse needs to push off in front of a jump, and when galloping they cause added stress on the hock and stifle joints.

Post-Legged/Straight Behind

DESCRIPTION:
When viewed from the side, the angles of the stifle and hock joints are open, with the entire limb appearing straight with minimal bends. The tibia is fairly vertical rather than having a more normal 60-degree slope.

HOW COMMON:
Common.

BREEDS/ACTIVITIES MOST AFFECTED:
This type of conformation is commonly seen in flat racing Thoroughbreds, steeplechase and timber horses, event horses, jumping horses, and hunters.

PERFORMANCE CONSEQUENCES:
• An understanding of limb mechanics dictates that the greater the horse's ability to straighten the leg, the better the speed of propulsion and the power of the thrust. The image often used to support this idea is an analogy of the swimmer pushing off the side of the pool as he executes a turn. In theory, a relatively straight hock facilitates forward and rearward reach as it opens and closes with a full range of motion without individual hock bones impinging on one another. This philosophy has led to selective breeding of speed horses with straight rear legs, particularly with long gaskins since the gaskin muscles impart acceleration.
• The problem with a post-legged horse is that this trait has been taken to the extreme. Tension on the hock joints irritates the joint capsule and joint cartilage, leading to bog spavin and bone spavin. Restriction of the Achilles tendon sheath while in motion leads to development of thoroughpin. The straightness of the stifle limits the excursion of the ligaments across the patella, predisposing these horses to upward fixation of the patella where the stifle joint sticks in a locked position. As well as interfering with performance, over time this can lead to degenerative arthritis of the stifle. Post-legged conformation makes it difficult for a horse to effectively use its lower back thereby reducing power and the swing of the leg; both features are important to speed and to an elastic stride.
• The rapid thrust of the rear limbs of post-legged horses causes the feet to stab into the ground, leading to foot bruising or quarter cracks.

MANAGEMENT/TRAINING STRATEGIES:
Care must be taken to adequately condition the whole horse to the task at hand to ease muscular effort and to develop endurance that will reduce fatigue. Exercises directed at development of the back and abdominal muscles further relieve work of the rear end.

BEST JOB FOR THIS HORSE:
Speed events like racing, steeplechase or timber racing, polo, eventing.

Left: In a horse that is straight behind, the angles at the stifle and hock are quite open. In theory this allows the horse to open and close with full range of motion without the hock bones interfering with each other.

Left: Historically, the horse that is straight behind has been favored for such sports as polo, racing, and jumping. In theory such a horse will have good speed and propulsion although problems arise from the straightness.

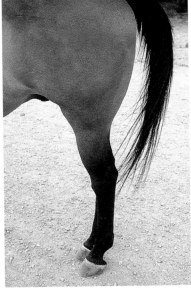

Above: A horse that is post-legged like this one is too straight behind and this conformation will cause injuries to the joint capsules and joint cartilage that can lead to bog spavin, bone spavin, and stifle arthritis.

Above: This jumper is quite straight behind, and notice how the open angle is exaggerated as he pushes off the ground.

Photo by Nancy S. Loving, DVM

181

Bow-Legged/Wobbly Hocks

DESCRIPTION:
As viewed from the rear, the hocks deviate away from each other to fall outside a plumb line dropped from the point of the buttocks.

HOW COMMON:
Uncommon.

BREEDS/ACTIVITIES MOST AFFECTED:
Quarter Horse types with bulldog stance.

PERFORMANCE CONSEQUENCES:
• In flight, the hoof wings in as the horse picks up its hocks and then rotates them out, predisposing to interference injury. The inward rotation described by the movement of the hocks leads to excess stress on the lateral hock structures, predisposing to bone spavin, bog spavin, and thoroughpin. In addition, the twisting motion of the hocks causes a screwing motion of the foot as it hits the ground, leading to foot bruising, corns, and quarter cracks particularly of the outside of the hoof, as well as to ringbone of the pastern or coffin joints.
• A bow-legged horse does not reach well forward with its hind limbs not only because of wasted motion caused by the twisting of the hocks as they are lifted, but also because the legs may not clear the abdomen if the stifles are directed more forward than normal. This reduces efficiency for speed or power limiting excellence in racing or jumping activities.

MANAGEMENT/TRAINING STRATEGIES:
Rear foot support with egg bar shoes will provide a solid support for limb thrust and minimize twisting of the lower joints and feet.

BEST JOB FOR THIS HORSE:
Light pleasure riding.

Far Left: This horse's hind legs bow out instead of landing straight. As he moves, his feet wing out, causing extra stress on the hoof, which will twist with each step.

Left: The inward rotation of legs while moving can make a horse with this conformation susceptible to bone spavin, bog spavin and thoroughpin.

Above: If in addition to being bow-legged a horse's stifles are directed more forward than normal, his legs may not clear his abdomen as he moves. This will limit his ability for disciplines like show jumping that require power and speed.

Cow Hocks/Medial Deviation of the Hocks/ Tarsus Valgus

DESCRIPTION:
As viewed from the rear, the hocks deviate in toward each other, with the cannon and fetlock placement well to the outside of the hocks. This gives the appearance of a half-moon contour from the stifle to the foot. Sickle-hocks often accompanies this conformational characteristic.

HOW COMMON:
Fairly common.

BREEDS/ACTIVITIES MOST AFFECTED:
Seen commonly in draft horse breeds. Disadvantageous to trotting horses, harness racers, jumping horses, speed events, and stock work.

PERFORMANCE CONSEQUENCES:
• The normal hock points slightly to the outside rather than dead ahead simply because the stifles must point slightly outward to be able to swing past the belly wall. Many times Arabians, Trakehners, and horses of Arabian descent are considered to have cow hocks, but if the fetlocks are in alignment beneath the hocks, these are not considered true cow hocks. Some slight inward turning of the hocks is not considered a conformational defect and should have no effect on performance. However, a horse with a very round barrel will be forced to turn its stifles more outward leading to an exaggerated cow-hocked appearance.
• Medial deviation of the hocks seen with true cow hocks places a tremendous amount of strain on the inside structures of the hock joints, predisposing the horse to bone spavin. In addition, an abnormal twisting motion of the pastern and cannons created by cow hocks predisposes the fetlocks to injury. More weight is carried on the medial aspect of the hooves, so bruising, corns, and quarter cracks are likely. The lower legs twist beneath the hocks as they land so interference injury of the lower legs is possible.
• A horse with cow hocks also only develops a relatively weak thrust, so speed often suffers.

MANAGEMENT/TRAINING STRATEGIES:
These horses need adequate rear foot support like egg bar shoes to provide a solid platform for foot placement and to minimize the twisting action of the hoof as the foot contacts the ground.

BEST JOB FOR THIS HORSE:
Low-speed, pleasure riding or driving.

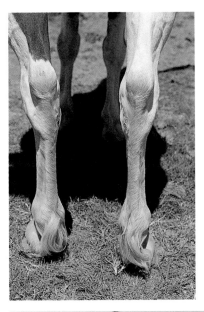

Cow hocks are hocks that lean in toward each other when a horse is standing squared up, with the fetlock well to the outside.

As this horse trots he is placing more weight on the outer portion of his hooves and legs. A cow-hocked horse puts excess strain as well on the inside of the hock joints. Such horses do best in egg bar shoes that help to lessen the amount the hoof twists as the foot hits the ground.

Stands Close Behind/Base-Narrow Behind

DESCRIPTION:
As viewed from behind in the ideal rear limb, a plumb line dropped from the point of the buttocks bisects the leg into two equal parts. A horse that is base-narrow behind has the lower legs and feet placed more toward the midline than the regions of the thigh and hips, with the plumb line falling to the outside of the lower leg from the hock down. This is often accompanied by a bow-legged conformation.

HOW COMMON:
Fairly common.

BREEDS/ACTIVITIES MOST AFFECTED:
Particularly affects heavily muscled horses like Quarter Horse types.

PERFORMANCE CONSEQUENCES:
• Base-narrow conformation behind has similar inherent problems as the horse that is base-narrow in front, i.e. with limb movement, the hooves tend to wing inward potentially creating interference injury to the opposite leg. Hocks that touch may also interfere with each other. The horse is not able to develop speed or rapid acceleration.
• The outside structures of the hock joints, fetlock joints, and hooves receive an excessive degree of stress and pressure. This leads to degenerative joint disease, ligamentous strain, hoof bruising, and quarter cracks.

MANAGEMENT/TRAINING STRATEGIES:
Care must be taken that the inside branches of the shoes do not hang to the side of the hoof as this will tend to amplify interference injuries to the ankles and lower legs.

BEST JOB FOR THIS HORSE:
Non-speed sports; sports that do not depend on spins, dodges, or tight turns used in stock work.

Base-Narrow problems in the hind legs are similar to those found in the front legs. The horse will tend to wing his feet inward as he lifts them and in so doing can injure the inside of his legs.

Conformation and Performance

Balance

Withers Higher than Croup

DESCRIPTION:
The peak of the withers is higher than the peak of the croup when the horse is squared up on a level surface.

HOW COMMON:
Common.

BREEDS/ACTIVITIES MOST AFFECTED:
Can affect any breed or sport.

PERFORMANCE CONSEQUENCES:
• The saddle tends to slide back toward the loins, moving the rider's center of gravity backward which makes it hard to maintain position and balance. The horse's lower back and loins may become sore from carrying a rider's weight in an area not well designed to do so. The girth moving back may interfere with the horse's chest capacity for breathing.
• A horse with this conformation assumes more weight on the hind end due to this uphill balance, which poses a greater risk to strain of the joints and ligaments of the rear legs, particularly of the stifles.

MANAGEMENT/TRAINING STRATEGIES:
Use a breast collar to hold the saddle from sliding toward the loins. Exercise on level ground that helps maintain the saddle in a proper position. Strengthening of haunches, back, and abdominal muscles minimizes risk of musculoskeletal strain.

BEST JOB FOR THIS HORSE:
With a well-fitting saddle, a horse with this characteristic can perform any sport but may work more comfortably in athletics ridden on level ground, such as equitation, dressage, pleasure riding, and racing.

As you can see in this side view, this horse's withers sit higher than his croup, which is a desirable difference. If the withers were any higher, this conformation could cause the saddle to slip backwards.

Use of a breast collar like this will help hold the saddle in place. Otherwise the rider will be behind the horse's center of balance and the horse's back and loins will take extra strain.

A horse with this "uphill" conformation carries more weight in his hind end and is at greater risk of straining the joints and ligaments of the hind legs, particularly the stifles.

Withers Lower than Croup/Rump High/ Downhill Balance

DESCRIPTION:
The peak of the croup is higher than the peak of the withers when the horse is squared up on a level surface.

HOW COMMON:
Uncommon.

BREEDS/ACTIVITIES MOST AFFECTED:
Affects any breed, especially Thoroughbreds. Affects all performance sports.

PERFORMANCE CONSEQUENCES:
• When the croup is higher than the withers the horse's weight shifts more onto the forehand, which reduces a horse's front-end agility. This has its greatest impact on horses performing gymnastic movements like dressage, jumping, reining, or cutting. The horse's muscles must work harder to continually "lift" the forehand, leading to more rapid muscular fatigue. Downhill balance also makes it more difficult for a jumping horse to raise its forehand at the base of a jump for liftoff. At speed, a downhill balanced horse feels more work on the muscles of the front legs and on the back and loin muscles in its efforts to lift its forelimbs from the ground.
• The downhill balance vastly increases concussion on the front legs, increasing the risk of musculoskeletal injury and forelimb lameness. The rider will feel a greater jar and impact from the horse's weight jamming its front end movement.
• A rump-high conformation tends to throw the saddle and rider forward toward the shoulders, leading to chafing from girth and saddle friction and to pressure around the withers. Shoulder movement is restricted by interference from the saddle and rider.
• Young horses up until age 3–4 may reach a stage in their growth where the rump is higher than the withers despite ultimately achieving perfect conformation (withers and croup are of equal heights). Growth spurts come and go as the horse matures, causing this phenomenon to intermittently reoccur.

MANAGEMENT/TRAINING STRATEGIES:
The horse needs powerful loins and strong abdominal muscles, sloping shoulders, and lightness of movement on the forehand to compensate for the downhill balance. The slope of the shoulders is dictated by conformation, but the loin and belly muscles can be strengthened with collected work, hill climbs, trotting and cantering cavallettis and jumping grids. A crupper may be needed to hold the saddle in place so it doesn't slide forward.

BEST JOB FOR THIS HORSE:
Pleasure riding, light trail riding, flat racing.

Right: The withers on this horse sit lower than his croup and this conformation puts extra weight on the front legs. A saddle will tend to slip forward toward the withers and can cause chafing and soreness.

Below: A high-rumped horse benefits from exercises like hill climbs, which will strengthen the loins and abdominal muscles. A crupper may be needed to hold the saddle in place.

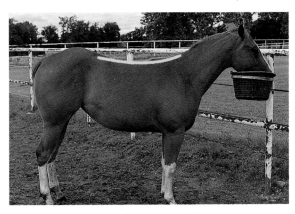

Above: The extra front-end weight makes it much harder for such a horse to "lift" its front feet. Sports like dressage are most affected.

Left: The added stress on the front legs brings greater risk of lameness and injury. Cutting is not the ideal sport for a horse that is rump high.

Too Tall (in context with rider)

DESCRIPTION:
The tall height of the horse is disproportionate to the size and length of leg of a short rider.

HOW COMMON:
Uncommon.

BREEDS/ACTIVITIES MOST AFFECTED:
Warmbloods, draft horses, Thoroughbreds.

PERFORMANCE CONSEQUENCES:
• When a horse is too tall for its rider the ability of the rider to communicate with seat and leg aids is affected. A very tiny rider on a very large Warmblood horse may be unable to initiate sensitive response to the aids. At the same time, the rider appears slightly ridiculous and out of context with the overall picture the horse presents.
• A tall horse is often not as handy or agile as a small, tightly coupled horse. This may affect coordination and agility in sports that require rapid changes in direction or terrain, like polo, reining, cutting, and trail riding.

MANAGEMENT/TRAINING STRATEGIES:
The sensible thing to do is for a rider to purchase a horse compatible with his or her size. Sometimes two different riders with two different builds ride the same horse, so the horse should be fitted to the larger rider.

BEST JOB FOR THIS HORSE:
The horse can do anything as long as the rider feels comfortable and is secure in the ability to control the horse.

Like the proverbial Goldilocks who wanted her porridge just right, you want to be mounted on a horse that fits your size. This rider clearly needs to grow into her mount.

When a rider is too small for her mount, her effectiveness as she uses her aids diminishes. Here, the rider's legs will be of little use since they barely touch the horse's sides.

Too Short (in context with rider)

DESCRIPTION:
The rider is disproportionately larger than his or her mount.

HOW COMMON:
Common.

BREEDS/ACTIVITIES MOST AFFECTED:
Arabians, Spanish Barbs, Paso Finos, Morgans, small Quarter Horses, ponies.

PERFORMANCE CONSEQUENCES:
• A large rider with long legs on a small horse can interfere with the athletic ability of the horse:
  1. The horse may not be able to maintain its balance due to the top-heavy, weighted effect of the rider sitting vertically in the saddle. The horse may be prone to tripping or falling if the rider loses a balanced seat position. 2. The heaviness of the rider in proportion to the horse's mass can lead to soreness of the back and loins, and to rapid muscle fatigue in general, reducing stamina. 3. The horse may be unwilling to jump or run fast due to the extreme work effort required to carry a large rider on its back. Despite the fact that small horses tend to be very agile and big-boned horses are strong for their size, a large rider forces the horse to overuse its muscles while the front limbs receive an excess of strain and impact with risk of developing lameness problems.
• A small horse makes it difficult for the rider to find a point of balance as the rider's legs barely contact the horse's relatively narrow sides. This makes it hard for the rider to effectively use leg aids for dressage and jumping cues, or for reining and cutting work.

MANAGEMENT/TRAINING STRATEGIES:
The only solution to this problem is for the rider to invest in a larger horse. For ideal musculoskeletal efficiency, a horse should carry less than 20 percent of its body weight. As an example, a 900-pound horse should carry a maximum of 180 pounds of combined weight of rider and tack.

BEST JOB FOR THIS HORSE:
Light pleasure riding; non-speed and non-jumping sports, and sports that don't require quick changes in direction or speed (i.e. not reining, cutting, barrel racing, polo, endurance racing).

This rider is much too tall for his mount. Notice how his legs hang below the horse's abdomen.

Photo by Nancy S. Loving, DVM

Having a rider that is too tall can make the horse top heavy. If the rider loses her balance, the horse is also likely to be thrown off balance and may trip or fall.

When the horse is too small for the rider, it is hard to use the leg aids correctly, particularly in dressage, cutting and reining, where leg contact is critical to engage the hind end.

Light-Framed/Fine-Boned

DESCRIPTION:
The substance of the long bones is slight and thin relative to the size and mass of the horse. This is especially noted in the area of the cannon bone and pastern.

HOW COMMON:
Common.

BREEDS/ACTIVITIES MOST AFFECTED:
Show horses, especially halter horses in non-performance work; Paso Finos; Gaited horses; Thoroughbreds. Affects longevity in any sport activity.

PERFORMANCE CONSEQUENCES:
• Refer to the section on Insufficient Bone for detail on the consequences of a light frame relative to a large size horse. Fine bones don't provide adequate support for the bulky musculature and at the same time create a visual impression of lack of overall harmony of body parts.
• In theory, a lighter frame reduces the weight on the end of the limbs making it easier for a horse to pick up each leg to sail across the ground. However, with a lot of speed work and impact stress, the light bones suffer concussion injury leading to bucked shins, splints, and stress fractures. The tendons, ligaments, and muscles have less of a lever system to pull across to effectively use or develop muscle strength for power and stamina.

MANAGEMENT/TRAINING STRATEGIES:
Match the light framed horse with a petite and lean rider.

BEST JOB FOR THIS HORSE:
Light pleasure or trail riding, driving in harness, non-impact and non-speed work.

Although he is well-muscled, this horse is light-framed. A lighter frame makes it easier for a horse to pick up his feet so he may appear to be sailing across the ground like this, but the impact on the lighter bones may lead to stress fractures and other leg injuries.

A light-framed horse is well suited to carriage work because he does not have the added weight of a rider, but also because the light-framed look adds a certain character preferred in driving sports.

Coarse-Boned/Sturdy-Framed

DESCRIPTION:
The long bones are big, wide, and strong in a horse with either a light muscled appearance or a bulky muscled horse.

HOW COMMON:
Common.

BREEDS/ACTIVITIES MOST AFFECTED:
Quarter horses, Arabians, draft horses, ponies, Morgans, Warmblood breeds. Advantageous to any performance activity.

PERFORMANCE CONSEQUENCES:
• Coarse-boned horses tend to be rugged and durable, and quite capable of carrying large weights relative to their size. With good conformation, such a horse should be quite agile in any sport, and hold up well to years of persistent athletic use.
• Big, solid bones provide strong levers for the muscles to pull against to improve efficiency of motion. This minimizes the effort of exercise and reduces the likelihood of developing fatigue, contributing to excellent endurance. The large bones may add to the mass of each leg the horse needs to lift and consequently slightly hinder speed at the gallop as applied to flat racing.

MANAGEMENT/TRAINING STRATEGIES:
Condition the horse to its maximum cardiovascular and musculoskeletal potential, and ride to the horse's current level of fitness. This will maintain athletic longevity.

BEST JOB FOR THIS HORSE:
Distance trail riding, jumping, eventing, steeplechasing and timber racing, reining, cutting, polo, roping, gymkhana, barrel racing, harness racing, driving in harness.

Left: A horse that is big-boned and well muscled such as this one can enjoy a long career in almost any sport.

Below Left:Big bones act as strong levers to pull a horse's muscles and enable him to move with great efficiency. Such a horse when well conditioned will have the staying power needed for endurance riding.

Left: To get the best mileage out of a well-built horse condition him to his potential in terms of strength and stamina.

Photo by Nancy S. Loving, DVM

Photo by Nancy S. Loving, DVM

Left: Endurance driving is no problem for the coarse-boned horse. He is rugged and durable and is able to pull heavy weights relative to his size.

Conformation and Performance

Movement Definitions

BRUSHING
Light contact of any form of scalping (see entry) constitutes brushing, where no actual injury may occur but hairs may be worn away with persistent occurrence.

COCKS HEAD TO ONE SIDE/CARRIES ONE EAR LOW
This type of head or ear carriage may result from incorrect training that has developed neck, poll, and mouth resistance in the horse, or it may result from injury to the neck, pain in the temporomandibular joint, pain in the mouth from dental problems, ticks in the ear, or damage to nerves supplying the ear. A source of disease or injury should be evaluated by a veterinarian, and once no pathologic problem has been discerned, correction can be made to improve suppleness and flexibility of the neck and poll, and to improve acceptance of bit contact.

CROSS-FIRING/CROSS-CANTERING
In true terms, cross-firing is seen in pacing horses where the inside of the hind foot contacts the inside of the front foot on the diagonal leg, e.g., LR contacts RF.

DAISY CLIPPER
The feet are barely lifted high enough to clear the ground. When this is coupled with efficient movement, the horse is very agile and maneuverable. When coupled with a weak, lazy movement, the horse is prone to tripping and stumbling.

DRAGS TOES
Just as the term states, the horse drags its toes, most typically on the rear limbs. This is evident by the wear marks on the front face of the rear toes. Often this occurs due to bone spavin which may be caused by conformational abnormalities such as cow hocks, sickle hocks, post-leggedness, or bandy legs.

FORGING
The toe of the hind foot slaps the sole or the bottom of the shoe of the front foot on the same side, creating a metallic clicking noise like the sound of a hammer tapping on an anvil.

GAITING/GAITEDNESS
Gaiting refers to the running walk, fox trot, amble, and rack (singlefoot). Each gait has its own characteristic and speed, but in each, the legs on the same side of the body move as lateral pairs much like a pace instead of the diagonal legs supporting the horse as seen at a trot. The differences between each "gait" lies in the difference in time between front and rear limb contact with the ground, and the height at which each leg is picked up. Gaiting imparts a smooth back movement that makes it easy for a rider to sit still in the saddle. Gaited horses often have long backs and loins which tend to ventroflex (hollow); this elevates the head and shoulders upward, making it easier for the horse to gait.

HEAD/NECK TOO LOW

In decades past, the hunter equitation world found a low-set neck with low head and neck carriage to be desirable in the show ring as it gave a "relaxed," steady appearance to the horse. Breeders went overboard with this idea and ended up breeding horses who move very heavily on the forehand, daisy-clip to the extreme, and have complete loss of agility, maneuverability, and speed. Fortunately, this conformational tendency is being culled from breeding stock to bring us back more athletic animals.

HIGH ACTION/HIGH MOTION IN FRONT

The horse's knees are lifted high into the air giving the appearance of "snap" and animation. This movement is favored by show, parade, and carriage horse events. This can be heritable through conformation, or trained with devices such as weighted shoes, ankle weights, and amplified by allowing the hooves and toes to grow overly long.

High action in front reduces the extension of the foreleg and in so doing reduces stride length in front so the horse has to modify travel behind, often falling out of balance. This makes it difficult for the horse to collect and use back and abdominal muscles. Excess strain and impact is placed on rear and front end joints, predisposing the horse to degenerative joint disease, sore front feet, sore back and loin muscles, and early fatigue.

HIGH MOTION BEHIND

Similar to high action in front, the horse snaps the hocks and stifles upward. This creates a flashy gait, but is often associated with conformational problems like sickle hocks, cow hocks, and bandy legs.

INTERFERING

The hoof of one leg swings inward to strike the opposite leg below the knee or hock, leading to a traumatic injury to soft tissues or bone or to a wound on the inner aspect of the opposite leg. This phenomenon is common in toed-out horses and in base-narrow horses, or may occur if a horse loses its balance or needs to suddenly shift its body or change direction.

NOT TRACKING UP

This term refers to a horse that does not step under itself with the rear legs. This can occur due to any of the following:
1. Pain in one or both hind limbs. 2. Pain in the back or loins. 3. Pain in one or both of the front limbs that restricts shoulder swing and necessarily shortens the rear leg stride. A horse that does not "track up" does not necessarily have an abnormal conformational characteristic, but it is harder for the horse to flex at the lumbosacral joint to properly engage the hindquarters in collection.

OVERREACHING

Due to an overly long stride behind or asynchronous movement between front and hind legs, the toe of the rear hoof strikes the rear of the front foot usually on the heel bulb. If the rear toe grabs the back of the front shoe, it will pull the shoe off.

OVERSTEPPING

The rear foot is placed forward beyond the imprint of the fore footprint. This is an asset since stride length is long and the horse covers ground more quickly with fewer steps and less muscular effort. This makes for efficient movement and a comfortable ride.

PADDLING

The hoof in flight "paddles" outward to the side giving the visual impression of busy lower leg movement. The rotational forces on the lower joints predispose to ringbone. This movement is commonly seen in toed-in horses.

PLAITING/ROPE WALKING

The foot travels an inward arc as the horse moves forward, but then the horse sets the foot down directly in line with the opposite front leg. This is commonly seen with horses with a base-narrow, toed-out conformation or with horses with shoulders that extend out in front of a narrow breast. This movement predisposes a horse to interference injuries, and to tripping and stumbling over its own feet.

PONY-GAITED/SHORT-STRIDED

Short, choppy steps occur in horses with steep, upright shoulders coupled with short, horizontal arm bones, and also in horses with upright pasterns. Short striding is also associated with pain in the front limb, most noticeably in the feet. Small-footed horses tend to have a greater tendency to develop navicular syndrome which makes the heels very sore. However, an injury at any level of the front leg will cause a horse to shorten its stride in one or more legs.

REFUSES TO TURN TO ONE SIDE

Resistance to bending to one side can result from pain in the mouth, neck, shoulders, thorax, or back that limits movement of the horse. Likewise, such resistance may be a learned behavior as the horse braces against incorrectly applied aids.

SCALPING

At fast trotting speeds, it is possible for the toe of the horse's front foot to "scalp" the front of the coronary band, pastern, or cannon region on the hind leg on the same side. The rear limb is moving forward, while the front limb on that same side extends rearward where they may contact each other.

SPEEDY CUTTING
Any type of interference from any limb to any other limb while the horse is traveling at fast speeds.

STARGAZER
A horse that carries the head and neck held high and in an extended position is referred to as a stargazer. Usually, this accompanies a ewe-necked conformation, but may be seen in any horse. The result is overdevelopment of the muscles on the underside of the neck so they bulge, and a sunken crest on the topside of the neck. Additionally, such a horse moves in a completely disjointed frame, with back and abdominal muscles poorly developed.

STRINGHALT
Stringhalt is an exaggerated and involuntary flexion of one or both rear legs toward the belly as the horse moves off at a walk, backs up, or turns. The cause of the problem is often related to injury to a nerve or tendon supplying the area of the hock, often following a traumatic injury. However, some cases of stringhalt may be related to toxicity problems associated with ingestion of certain plants.

STUMBLING
A horse that stumbles fails to pick up the front feet to fully lift them clear of the ground. This often occurs due to foot soreness that makes the horse less eager to pick up or land on the foot. Such a phenomenon is commonly seen in horses with navicular disease or laminitis, but poor shoeing, stone bruises, corns, or long toes will also cause a horse to stumble.

UNCOORDINATED/PROPRIOCEPTIVE DEFECT
Any uncoordinated movement may be associated with pain or with neurologic disease and is cause for considerable concern to the horse owner. Uncoordinated movements often suggest an underlying problem with proprioception (the ability of the horse to recognize spatial position of each limb) that could foretell Wobbler syndrome. This is a neurologic disease caused by impingement of the spinal cord in restricted and narrowed vertebral spaces and is sometimes associated with necks that are very slender at the top toward the throatlatch. Other neurologic problems arise with trauma, equine protozoal myelitis (EPM), and equine motor neuron disease, to name a few.

WINGING
The hoof in flight swings inward with the potential to create interference injury. This is commonly seen in toed-out conformation.

Glossary

ANGULAR LIMB DEFORMITY (ALD):
Abnormal alignment of the long bones due to differences in growth rate of each side of the growth plate; this results in a toed-out or toed-in stance.

BLEEDER:
See Exercise-Induced Pulmonary Hemorrhage.

BOG SPAVIN:
Distention of the tibiotarsal joint of the hock with extra production of joint fluid related to low-grade inflammation or chronic irritation.

BONE SPAVIN:
Osteoarthritis of the hock joints, often accompanied by lameness. Visible signs may be apparent as a bony enlargement over the inside aspect of the hock.

BOWED TENDON:
Strain or tearing of a flexor tendon on the back of the cannon area. Inflammation and scar tissue repair may result in a thickened, "bowed" appearance once healed.

BUCKED SHINS:
Pain develops along the front of the cannon bones of the front legs; related to constant irritation commonly associated with training at fast speeds.

CARDIOVASCULAR:
Relating to the system of the heart and blood vessels.

CAUDAL:
Toward the rear.

CERVICAL VERTEBRAL MALFORMATION:
See Wobbler Syndrome.

CORNS:
Pressure of the sole at the angle formed by the wall and the bar may lead to pain and lameness.

CURB:
Strain and inflammation of the plantar ligament on the outside of the rear lower area of the hock leads to an enlargement in that area.

DEGENERATIVE ARTHRITIS:
Refer to Degenerative Joint Disease.

DEGENERATIVE JOINT DISEASE (DJD):
Also referred to as osteoarthritis, osteoarthrosis, or degenerative arthritis, this condition is a progressive deterioration of structures within a joint—particularly of the joint cartilage—ultimately leading to changes in the bone and soft tissues of the joint.

DESMITIS:
Inflammation or strain of a ligament.

DEVELOPMENTAL ORTHOPEDIC DISEASE (DOD):
A number of bone disease processes of growing young horses such as epiphysitis, osteochondrosis, osteochondritis dessicans, and angular limb deformities.

DISTAL:
Relating to lower, or toward the bottom.

DORSAL DISPLACEMENT OF THE SOFT PALATE:
The soft palate lodges over the top of the epiglottis (opening of the larynx) and obstructs normal airflow.

EPIGLOTTIC ENTRAPMENT:
One of the cartilages of the larynx becomes entrapped in a loose fold of mucous membrane originating from the floor of the mouth.

EQUINE MOTOR NEURON DISEASE:
Degenerative neurologic disease affecting the peripheral nerves causing muscular trembling and atrophy.

EQUINE PROTOZOAL MYELITIS (EPM):
A neurologic disease caused by a protozoal parasite that damages the central nervous system as it migrates through the spinal cord. An affected horse shows an asymmetric gait irregularity, focal muscle atrophy, and ataxia (incoordination).

EXERCISE-INDUCED PULMONARY HEMORRHAGE (EIPH):
Bleeding of the lungs related to high-speed exercise. Often referred to as a "bleeder."

HIGH RINGBONE:
Degenerative joint disease of the pastern joint.

HUMERUS:
Arm bone.

HYPERTROPHY:
Overdeveloped or enlarged.

JIBBAH:
Bulge of the forehead.

LAMINITIS:
Inflammation of the laminae of the foot arising from concussion trauma or metabolic disorders. Laminitis accompanied by rotation of the coffin bone results in debilitating and career-threatening lameness.

LATERAL:
Relating to the outside.

LOW RINGBONE:
Degenerative joint disease of the coffin joint.

LUMBAR:
Area of the lower back.

LUMBO-SACRAL:
Junction of the lower back with the pelvis where the lumbar vertebrae meet the sacrum.

MASTICATION:
Chewing.

MEDIAL:
Relating to the inside or toward the middle.

MUSCULOSKELETAL:
Relating to the muscles and nerves and their interaction.

NAVICULAR SYNDROME:
Inflammation of the navicular bone, navicular bursa, and/or of the deep digital flexor tendon where it passes behind the navicular bone. Lameness relates to the horse being sore in its heels, with a characteristic toe stabbing or pony-strided gait, particularly noted on hard terrain, uneven terrain, and on descents.

OSTEOARTHRITIS:
Refer to Degenerative Joint Disease.

OSTEOARTHROSIS:
Refer to Degenerative Joint Disease.

QUARTER CRACKS:
A crack in the hoof wall in the area of the heel or rear quarter of the foot.

RADIUS:
Forearm bone.

RECURRENT LARYNGEAL NEUROPATHY:
Partial or complete paralysis of the recurrent laryngeal nerve causes the laryngeal cartilage to remain collapsed in the airway, resulting in a roaring noise from turbulence of air intake with breathing.

RUN-DOWN INJURY:
Wounds or strain of the structures on the rear of the fetlock.

SAND CRACKS:
Fissures in the hoof wall that are related to weak and brittle hoof horn. Often associated with thin walls and/or a long toe, low heel hoof configuration.

SCOPE:
The degree of freedom and range of motion of the limbs while in motion. A scopey horse is one that is able to crouch low during stock work, fold its legs tightly over a jump, or extend its legs in a big, free-flowing trot.

SESAMOIDITIS:
Inflammation of the sesamoid bone along the back of the fetlock joint.

SHEARED HEELS:
One heel bulb is pushed up higher than the other heel bulb due to chronic hoof imbalances. This instability of the heels often leads to heel pain and lameness, and thrush.

SIDEBONES:
Calcification of one or both collateral cartilages of the foot. Usually a sidebone is not associated with lameness unless the calcification fractures.

SPLINTS:
Inflammation along the small splint bone (second metacarpal or metatarsal bone) that lies alongside the cannon bone may result in a visible bony proliferation around the injured area.

THOROUGHPIN:
A windpuff or fluid distention of the Achille's tendon above the hock joint.

THRUSH:
Infection of the frog accompanied by black debris and a foul odor. If degeneration of the frog invades sensitive tissues, the horse may become lame.

UPWARD FIXATION OF THE PATELLA:
The medial patellar ligament catches over the femur locking the patella in place. This results in an intermittent locking of the stifle in extension so the leg cannot flex. Often associated with post-legged conformation.

WINDGALL:
See Windpuffs.

WINDPUFFS:
Distention of a joint or tendon sheath with excess fluid due to chronic irritation or strain. Also referred to as a windgall.

WOBBLER SYNDROME:
A narrowing of the spinal canal of the cervical vertebrae places compression on the spinal cord, resulting in neurologic abnormalities, incoordination, proprioception difficulties, muscle weakness, and unsteadiness. Also referred to as cervical vertebral malformation.

Conformation and Performance

Index

Base-wide horses, 116
Behind, 170, 176, 180, 186, 204
Bending exercises, 20, 52
"Bleeder," 12, 208
Bog spavin, 178, 180, 182, 207
Bone spavin, 178, 180, 182, 184, 203
Bones
  coarse, 200
  fine, 198
  heavy, large, 100
  insufficient, 100, 198
  See also type of bone
Breast, 88, 90, 116, 205
Breastplate, 36
Broodmares, 54, 156
Brushing, 203
Buttocks, 152, 176, 182

C
Cannon bone
  and behind, 176
  and feet, 205
  and fetlock, 126
  and forearm, 92
  and frames and bones, 198
  and gaskin, 168, 170
  and hocks, 168, 170, 174, 178, 184
  and insufficient bone, 100
  and knees, 102, 106
  and legs, 178
  long, 96, 168
  offset, 106
  and pasterns, 110, 112
  rotated, 124
  and scalping, 205
  short, 98
  See also Shins: bucked
Canter, 26, 50, 72, 126, 150, 162, 168, 170, 192, 203
Carpus, 98, 102, 104, 116, 122, 124
Carriage driving. *See* Driving in harness
Carriage. *See* Head; Tail
Cavalletti exercises
  and arm bone, 86
  and back, 50
  and breast, 88
  and croup, 192
  and downhill balance, 192
  and gaskin, 168
  and hips, 160, 162
  and hocks, 168
  and knees, 104, 108
  and rump, 152, 192
  and slab-sided, 72
  and thighs, 154
  and withers, 34, 192
Chest, 66, 68, 70, 72, 82

Coffin joints, 110, 120, 134, 140, 142, 182, 208
Colic, 20
Collars, 34, 68, 72, 190
Collection
  and arm bone, 84
  and back, 42, 50, 54, 76
  and croup, 56, 192
  and downhill balance, 192
  and hindquarters, 150
  and hunter's bump, 48
  and knees, 204
  and loins, 44
  and neck, 16, 24, 30
  and not tracking up, 204
  and rump, 152, 192
  and slab-sided, 72
  and wasp-waisted, 74
  and withers, 34, 36, 40, 192
Combined driving, 96, 110, 150
Compression fractures, 104
Conditioning
  and back, 54, 76
  and behind, 180
  and breast, 88
  and cannon bone, 96, 98, 124
  and chest, 66
  and face, 8
  and forearm, 92, 94
  and frames and bones, 200
  and hips, 158, 166
  and hocks, 174
  and hunter's bump, 48
  and insufficient bone, 100
  and jaw, 12
  and legs, 180
  and neck, 24, 28
  and nostrils, 10
  and pigeon-breast, 90
  and ribs, 66, 70
  and shoulder, 82
  and stifles, 166
  and thighs, 154
  and throatlatch, 12
  and vulva, 156
Control of horse, 24, 32, 194
Coordination, 44, 96, 194, 206, 209
Corns, 136, 142, 144, 182, 184, 206, 207
Coupling, 42, 44, 46, 70
Crest, 20, 24, 28, 30, 206
Cross-canter, 203
Cross-firing, 203
Crouching, 68, 90
Croup
  and back, 42, 54
  and coupling, 44
  flat or horizontal, 58, 60